HOMESPUN DEVOTIONS

VOLUME ONE

CHERYL E. SMITH

Copyright © 2021 by Cheryl E. Smith

All rights reserved. No part of this publication may be reproduced or transmitted in any form or by any means without written permission from the author. Unless otherwise indicated, all Scripture is taken from the King James Version of the Bible.

Special gratitude and acknowledgments:

Cover design by **Zachary Smith**

Cover image by **Racheal Cooper** @rachealcooperphotography.com

Formatting and technical assistance by **Kalen Bruce** @freedomsprout.com

First and foremost, I dedicate this book, my life, and my all to my Lord and Savior, Jesus Christ. To say I owe Him everything is an understatement of monumental proportions. Thank You, Jesus, from the bottom of my heart—I have never loved You more.

Secondly, I dedicate this book to my two fellow travelers on life's journey—my dear husband, Kevin, and our precious son, Zach. There are no two people with whom I would rather walk out my earthly pilgrimage. You are Aaron and Hur to me. Thank you for always standing by me, praying for me, lifting my arms in the battle, and encouraging me to keep pressing on. I love you both with more love than my heart can hold.

"A threefold cord is not quickly broken." Ecclesiastes 4:12

CONTENTS

Introduction	vii
1. Puzzles	1
2. Your First Love	5
3. Squirming Puppies	9
4. Ministering in the Shadows	12
5. Picky Eaters	16
6. Missing Dad	19
7. In His Image	22
8. More Grace	25
9. The Last Quail	29
10. Twenty-One Days	32
11. Storms in the Night	35
12. Superheroes	38
13. Broken Hearts	41
14. Elanore	45
15. Foggy Conditions	49
16. Sparrows	52
17. A Good Name	55
18. Windows of Opportunity	58
19. I Can Heal	61
20. Solitary Places	65
21. You Asked, Didn't You?	68
22. When Jesus Sees Us Weep	72
23. Lemons & Dirt	76
24. Empty Feeders	79
25. Never Alone	82
26. The Next Page	86
27. Forgotten Benefits	89
28. Digging Old Wells	92
29. Guard Rails	95
30. Our Footprints	99

31. Sister Rose	102
32. Resting with the Shepherd	105
33. Christmas from the Dumpster	108
34. The Power of Song	111
35. Princess	115
36. The Walking King James	118
37. My Symbol of Hope	122
38. Bentley's Rebellion	126
39. The Broken Ones	129
40. Angels & Sleepy Drivers	132
41. The Painting	135
42. Pass It on	138
43. The Benefits of Waiting	142
44. And Peter	146
45. No Junk	150
46. The Lord Remembers	154
47. The Strength of Horses	158
48. Together	161
49. Keeping Love Alive	164
50. Our Legacy	169

INTRODUCTION

Several years ago, my family and I had just walked through one of the most challenging trials of our lives. Having worked in church leadership for several years, then being called by God to leave that post of duty, I found myself in a very unfamiliar place, struggling to know what to do next. A short time later, my mother became seriously ill, and during her extended hospital stay, I sent out daily updates to family and friends who were praying for her. One day, while my Uncle Donnie and I were discussing all that was happening and how God's will seemed to be such a mystery, he said, "Cheryl, I've been sharing your daily emails with people at church, and it has been a blessing and encouragement to them. It is your gift. You need to write."

Write? Is that what God wanted me to do next? And, if so, how? I had been blessed with some success as a greeting card writer, had written songs and poetry and even an unpublished fictional Christian romance book, but did God want me to write full time? Was this to be my next phase of ministry and service to Him?

As I continued to seek the Lord's will, I kept hearing Uncle Donnie's voice encouraging me to use what was not only my God-given gift but was also something I had long dreamed of doing. It soon became apparent that God was leading me to start a blog called Homespun Devotions. I knew nothing about blogging, but He faithfully enabled me to establish a platform to continue ministering and sharing the many thoughts He places on my heart.

Over the next nearly ten years, I have continued writing and publishing those thoughts, shared family stories, and talked about the lessons God has taught my husband, Kevin, our son, Zachary, and me. A few months ago, the Lord began to lead me to pull most of those 800 plus posts off the blog and compile a portion of them into a series of books—50 devotionals per book. This is Volume One. Lord willing, and by God's grace, there will be more books to come, the number of which is known only to Him.

Interestingly, when I first started out blogging, my dream was not to blog but to write a book called "Homespun Devotions." All those days of pressing through and continuing to write when it felt so useless and less than the dream of writing a devotional book, God was having me do just that. Not just one book, but a series! All along, He knew. Zechariah 4:10 says, "For who hath despised the day of small things?" God often starts us off with a small portion of the larger plan and only reveals more to us as we are faithful in the little.

As I grew up, there were five cherished dreams in my girlhood heart: to follow Jesus, to be a wife, to be a mother, to write, and to sing.

Dream #1 comes true for me every day I live and breathe.

Being a disciple of Jesus brings the most profound sense of peace, and living a life of service to Him fulfills my heart's greatest desire.

Dream #2 came true the day I walked down the aisle, pledged my heart and hand, and married my best friend, Kevin—the man of my dreams, my soulmate, the love of my life.

Together, we thought Dream #3 would soon follow. God had other plans. Due to my health issues, we struggled with infertility for many years. The pain and anguish in the heart of a woman who cannot conceive are very familiar to me. Should you find yourself in that same struggle, I want to encourage you with these truths—God is still on His throne, and He still hears Hannah-like prayers.

After many years of praying like Hannah, God miraculously opened my barren womb, and He allowed Dream #3 to come true when He sent Kevin and me a healthy, beyond precious baby boy 12 ½ years after we were married. Zach continually blesses us and graces our lives and home with more love than our hearts can hold. I will forever be grateful for our 13-year homeschooling journey that began on his first day of Kindergarten and ended on the day of his graduation. The blessing of being Kevin's wife and Zach's mother is surpassed only by the joy of being God's child. All glory to Him for the immeasurable gifts of being a wife and mother.

Dream #4 comes true each time I pick up my laptop to write. My first published book, "Biblical Minimalism: Following Jesus from a Life of Abundance to a More Abundant Life," is the story of our family's journey of drawing closer to Jesus, letting go of excess, and becoming 100% debt-free.

My dream to sing comes true each time I pick up my guitar and belt out old, familiar songs from my childhood. Bluegrass music connects me to my past and keeps my feet on the ground. I never hear a five-string banjo without thinking of Dad and missing him and Mom so much it hurts. ***How I wish they were still here.***

I point you to no denomination, religious group, or sect—*only* to the foot of the cross of Jesus Christ, where redemption, restoration, healing, and peace still freely and lavishly flow. This book is holy living broken down into bite-sized pieces like quilt scraps—multicolored thoughts, stories, and lessons of the heart, homespun with love and stitched together by the common thread of the simplicity of the Gospel of Jesus Christ.

I hope you feel wrapped in comfort and are blessed and graced with His presence as you read.

1
PUZZLES

"And we know that all things work together for good to them that love God, to them who are the called according to His purpose." Romans 8:28

Romans 8:28 is sometimes misinterpreted and used as a license to "name and claim" prosperity, thriving health, and life that resembles perfection. The truth is, this type of utopia eludes those of us who may be far from prospering, whose bodies are pain-racked, and who are experiencing the fiery trials Peter spoke about in I Peter 4:12,13. "Beloved, think it not strange concerning the fiery trial which is to try you, as though some strange thing happened unto you: but rejoice, inasmuch as ye are partakers of Christ's sufferings; that when His glory shall be revealed, ye may be glad also with exceeding joy."

We get up every morning and face the reality that we live in a fallen world; life is full of struggles; body parts age, wear out, and malfunction; and there is a cross for each one of us that must be picked up and carried daily to follow Jesus Christ.

Romans 8:28 does not say that "all things that happen to those who love God will be good things," nor does it say, "If God calls you, you will only experience life's best." Contrariwise, it teaches us that God will allow the good, and He will permit the bad. Then He will weave all things together to produce a result that is ultimately good—something pieced together by His loving hand to bring about an "expected end."

"For I know the thoughts that I think toward you, saith the LORD, thoughts of peace, and not of evil, to give you an expected end." Jeremiah 29:11

Nothing had ever demonstrated Romans 8:28 more clearly to me than when God used a simple jigsaw puzzle to drive home the point.

At age 77, Mom was involved in a severe car accident, which resulted in an operation and extended stay in a rehabilitation facility. Every day, Zach and I would make the 30-mile trip to visit and spend time with her. Zach was little and easily amused, and bless his heart, he was and still is such a faithful, loyal trooper. Each day, he would crawl into Mom's hospital bed beside her, and together, the two of them would watch his favorite cartoons, snug as a bug in a rug for hours on end.

As for me, the hours went by slowly, so I bought jigsaw puzzles to pass the time. I would spread a puzzle out on cardboard at the foot of Mom's hospital bed and work on it through the day; then, when it came time for Zach and me to leave each evening, I would slide the puzzle and cardboard under her bed to resume the next day when we returned. After I finished one puzzle, I would begin another.

Each time I started a new puzzle, I dumped all the pieces onto the cardboard, and it looked like a jumbled mess. It was so confusing, in the beginning, when each piece was separate. I could only imagine that the mixed-up pieces in front of me would look just like the picture on the front of the box one day.

Some jigsaw puzzle pieces are unattractive and seem to have no point. Others are vibrantly colored, and you can instantly see that they are flowers, trees, faces, or something else meaningful. They immediately make sense and have a point, even though each piece is incomplete on its own.

Then one day, you set the final piece in place, and, suddenly, the purpose of each piece makes sense—even those pieces that were so unsightly and didn't seem to contribute anything valuable, necessary, or worthwhile.

Looking at the finished product, you no longer see a black piece here that is ugly or a bright piece there that is beautiful. What appeared to be misshapen and unseemly was the brim of a gentleman's hat or the hinge of an iron gate that opens to a stunning rose garden just beyond. What appeared to be foreboding shadows joined together to create the silver canopy of the carriage transporting the lady of the manor.

When the puzzle is completely assembled, it occurs to you that the pieces had to fall into place in a particular order. Piece A had to be inserted before piece B would have a place. Piece D would not fit properly until Piece C was attached to Piece B. You no longer see pieces at all but a completed picture—"an expected end" result. The whole. A culmination of hundreds of parts. Amazingly, it looks exactly like it is supposed to look. Seeing the finished product, you realize that every piece was woven together to create what it was intended to be all along—*something good.*

One day, it occurred to me that jigsaw puzzles are a lot like life.

God is in a continual process of working the puzzle pieces of our lives. Some of the pieces are dark, and we struggle to make any sense of them at all. Others are peaceful, lovely scenes that seem to make perfect sense, right from their onset. The older we become, the more we realize that the good and bad come in stages, and not every piece of our life's puzzle will be beautiful or fall into place in the time and way we think is best. Just as it takes time to assemble the hundreds, sometimes thousands, of jigsaw puzzle pieces, it takes time for God to "perfect that which concerns" us. (Psalm 138:8) We are a work in progress. He is the Master Builder, daily constructing the composition of "us" into the finished product "picture" He envisions us to be. One day, He will place that last piece in the empty spot, and we will hear the words, "Well done, thou good and faithful servant: enter thou into the joy of thy lord." Matthew 25:21

As we look at the individual pieces, life can seem so puzzling. On that day, when our puzzle is complete, we will stand awestruck in His holy presence. Every piece, ***including the ugly failures, dark disappointments, and unseemly defeats,*** will all fit perfectly together into one splendid embodiment of His foreknowledge, **and it will all make perfect sense.**

2

YOUR FIRST LOVE

"Nevertheless, I have somewhat against thee because thou hast left thy first love." Revelation 2:4

We were driving through the Everglades, across the lonely stretch of Alligator Alley that spans the distance between the east and west coasts of southern Florida. It was just Mom and me in the car, and I could tell she had something heavy on her mind that she needed to unload, so I listened close.

I was a teenager at the time, in that uncertain, not-sure-what-to-do-with-the-rest-of-my-life phase, and Mom was several years into her marriage with Dad. To say the two of them were not getting along well would be an understatement, and Mom was in a depressed and reflective state of mind.

I thought I knew all of Mom's life story—she married young and had my four siblings by her first husband, Eddie, he died a very sudden and tragic death, and Mom was left a widow and single mother at a young age. A few years later, she met and married Dad, and a little over a year later, I was born. I knew Mom had suffered other deep losses—both parents, her 15-year-old sister (when Mom was only 17), and one of her brothers. But the story she shared with me that afternoon was all new to me. I had never heard her talk about it before and wonder now if her and Dad's marital problems brought it all to the surface. Whatever the reason, she decided to revisit a very painful place in her past and take me along.

She started by telling me that you never forget your first love. I had always thought her first husband was her first love, so when she went on to talk of a guy named Norman, it came as a complete surprise. She had been young—only 17 or so, when she was introduced to Norman by her sister-in-law, Dorothy, who was married to Mom's brother, Paul.

Mom and Norman fell in love and talked of a future together, but Papaw disapproved of their relationship. After Papaw forbade Mom to continue seeing him, Norman joined the armed forces and was stationed far from home. In the months that followed, there was no contact between him and Mom, even though she made attempts to keep in touch, and she gave up on ever hearing from Norman again. She met Eddie, Papaw approved, and soon after Eddie and Mom were married, she became pregnant with my oldest sister, Sharon.

One day, engagement ring in hand, Norman unexpectedly came home from the service and went to Uncle Paul's and Aunt Dorothy's home, looking for Mom! Intending to ask her to marry him, I can only imagine how he felt when Aunt Dorothy told him Mom had already married someone else.

Not long after, as Mom was riding a bus downtown, she ran into Norman. Her heart ached as they stood and talked about what might have been. Mom was already unhappy in her marriage, and the temptation was strong to walk away and back into her interrupted relationship with Norman. I could tell by the way Mom talked that it was hard for her to do the right thing that day. Ultimately, she said goodbye to Norman and remained faithful to her wedding vows.

All those years, Mom had been silently bearing the hurt of having left her first love. So many times, after sharing her story with me that day, she talked about how different things could and would have been if she had followed her heart and waited.

After Dad died, I mustered the courage to ask Mom if she would mind if I tried to find Norman. I wanted to know where he was, how his life had turned out, and I hoped that maybe Mom could talk to him for old times' sake.

As I started searching for his name on the internet, I quickly found a few matches. At first, Mom was apprehensive and reluctant to think about talking to him again, but she finally agreed. She nervously began to call the phone numbers I came up with, and it turned out "her" Norman was the second one on my list.

After all those many years, they spoke again—Mom and her first love. She found out he had married and settled in Kentucky, and while speaking with Norman's wife, it was apparent she had heard all about Mom. Norman later wrote Mom a letter to catch up and tell her more about his life and adventures through the years.

One day, Mom called him again just to say hello. His wife answered the phone with sad news—Norman had suffered a heart attack and passed away. It seemed I saw a part of Mom die that day, too. What might have been? We will never know. We all make choices, and we live with the consequences, whatever they may be.

People leave their first love, move on, then deal with the haunting questions that follow.

Jesus told the church at Ephesus that they had left their first love. They were still a church-going crowd who looked like they had it all together on the outside, but inside they were void of their original love and passion for Jesus Christ. He was no longer number one.

Do you remember when you first met Jesus? Remember how your heart was "on fire" with passion and zeal? How you wanted to spend every possible second you could with Him, and how you couldn't wait to spend the rest of your life walking with Him hand in hand, doing all you could to serve and love Him more?

Do you still feel that way? Does your heart still yearn for time with Him? Or somewhere down the line, did you walk away? Did someone or something come in and steal His place in your heart? Is He still number one? Is He still your first love, or have you left Him?

He is still available, waiting for you to come back to Him. His love for you is endless and unconditional. He still wants to be first in your heart and life, and He is ready to forgive if you have strayed.

Psalm 86:5 says, "For thou, Lord, *art* good, and ready to forgive; and plenteous in mercy unto all them that call upon Thee." He is the God of second chances, and He allows U-turns. It won't take you long to find Him. All it takes is a sincere, heartfelt prayer of repentance. He will put the past behind you, and you can start again. Sadly, there was not a second chance for Mom and Norman. Thankfully, it is not too late for ***you and Jesus***.

3

SQUIRMING PUPPIES

"Trust in the Lord with all thine heart, and lean not unto thine own understanding. In all thy ways acknowledge Him, and He shall direct thy paths."
Proverbs 3:5,6

*N*ot long after Kevin and I were married, we visited my aunt and uncle, who lived out of town. Upon our arrival, we found out their neighbor's Chow had just had puppies. They were the cutest things, and by the time we left to come home, they had talked us into bringing two of them home with us!

We were living in an apartment without a fenced-in yard, and it did not take long for us to figure out that our puppies needed to be taught obedience—especially the female, whom we affectionately named Katie. She was full of spunk and strong-willed. She refused to cooperate and come to us when called, and she would take off on daring adventures that left us exhausted in our quest to bring her safely back home.

We had heard of a local obedience class for dogs, so we enrolled Katie and her brother, Teddy, and soon began our weekly classes. One of the exercises they taught us involved the all-important issue of trust and the valuable spiritual lesson it taught me concerning trusting God still lingers after all these years.

We were taught to hold the puppy on its back in the palms of our hands, forcing it to stay in that position until it stopped squirming. As crazy as it sounded, we began to try it at home. It came as no surprise when the puppies started to squirm and squeal and try every way possible to wiggle onto their feet away from the firmness of our grasp. Oh, how they squirmed! But no matter how hard they tried to get away from us, we would not give in. We forced them to stay on their back in our palms until the squirming stopped. The whole point of the exercise was to prove to the puppy that they were safe; we would not drop them or let them go under any circumstance; we were in control, and they had to succumb to our authority; they had to yield their will to ours. Needless to say, they didn't like this exercise—not even a little, and I hate to admit it, but when it comes to my ongoing quest to fully trust God, I am a whole lot like those squirming puppies.

Deuteronomy 33:27 says, "The eternal God is thy refuge, and underneath are the everlasting arms." Arms that have always been and always will be; arms that have enough power and strength to hold the world in place; arms that have picked me up countless times and held firm until the fear in me was stilled, and I stopped trembling; arms that have carried me across raging tempests and through fiery furnaces and over insurmountable mountains; arms that make me feel safe and loved and comforted.

How many times have the palms of God's hands had to keep me in an uncomfortable, vulnerable position until I stopped squirming? And when will I learn that as long as I continue to squirm and the more I complain and whine and grumble, the longer He will hold me there? It is all a matter of trust. If His everlasting arms are underneath me, and they have never let me go, why can't I trust Him now?

Even after all these years, I am far too often a lot like those insecure, terrified puppies. Recalling Teddy's and Katie's suspicion of us and their difficulty in learning that we had their best interests at heart, I can't help wondering how much I must frustrate the Lord when I doubt His ability to hold me fast. But I take heart as I remember the rest of the story.

Over time and with a lot of patience and consistency, those puppies finally learned that we were not going to drop them, nor were we going to let them go until they relaxed in our grasp. As they started to see that we would keep them safe and the only way they could escape was to stop squirming, a measure of trust was built and strengthened between us. They began to understand that they would be okay, even though they were not in control or standing independently on their own feet. It was quite an accomplishment to feel their tension and fear relax as they finally seemed to understand that we were worthy of their trust. There came a time when they did not squirm anymore—at least not nearly as often or as much.

So, I believe there is still hope for me. The other day, it hit me that I was just a bit more trusting while going through a severe test and trial. I realized I had consecrated the battle to the Lord a lot quicker than I used to. So, maybe I, like Teddy and Katie, am making progress in this issue of trust. Maybe one day, I won't squirm at all.

4

MINISTERING IN THE SHADOWS

"For if these things be in you, and abound, they make you that ye shall neither be barren nor unfruitful in the knowledge of our Lord Jesus Christ." 2 Peter 1:8

Do you feel spiritually handicapped by your current situation and unable to do what you would like to do for God? Did you know that at least five of Paul's epistles were written while imprisoned? Four of these were during his Roman imprisonment, in which he was permitted to live in his own hired house. He was under the scrutiny of the Roman guards when he penned the Ephesian, Philippian, Colossian, and Philemon letters and his second letter to Timothy. I wonder if he was watching one of those Roman guards pacing outside his window and possibly studying his armor when he wrote the mainstay "Armor of God" passage in Ephesians 6. Was he enduring some type of cruel treatment when the words "For to me to live is Christ, and to die is gain" (Philippians 1:21) were flowing through his pen? Did he feel the pangs of loneliness and abandonment when he said, "For though I be absent in the flesh, yet am I with you in the spirit..." in Colossians 2:5? Could he have been experiencing declining health when he called himself "Paul the aged" in the ninth verse of his letter to Philemon?

Chronologically, the last Bible letter the Apostle Paul wrote was to his special, spiritual "son," Timothy. He must have sensed that he was nearing the end of his life when he penned those famous words, "I have fought a good fight, I have finished my course, I have kept the faith: Henceforth there is laid up for me a crown of righteousness, which the Lord, the righteous judge, shall give me at that day: and not to me only, but unto all them also that love His appearing" in II Timothy 4:7,8.

When thinking of the Apostle Paul, many times, his public preaching is what first comes to mind. It is inspiring to think about the bold and powerful sermons he delivered in Damascus immediately after his conversion (Acts 9:20, 27), how he mightily brought forth the spoken Word of God in Salamis (Acts 13:5), the anointed truth he expounded at the invitation of the rulers of the Antioch synagogue (Acts 13:14-41), and how he continued to strongly proclaim the Gospel amid impending persecution (Acts 14:1-4).

But, what about the work God used him to do while he was alone, secluded, and obscure to the world around him? What about the letters he was writing that would go on to become major components of what we now call the New Testament? Wasn't his quiet work for God equally as important as the awe-inspiring work God wrought through him while preaching to the multitudes?

He may have felt frustrated, feeling the need to get out and speak loudly from places like Mars Hill (Acts 17:22) while being held under bondage to the prison of Rome. Maybe he thought the letters he was writing would reach their destination only to be discarded, never reaching anyone other than the ones to whom they were addressed. Could he have even imagined that there would one day be a book called the Bible, those very letters would be carefully preserved and included in God's holy Word, and countless followers of Jesus would build their entire lives on the teaching he was producing from those lonely places of isolation?

Where are you today? Are you laid aside through some physical disability? Do you long to be out "on the battlefield" for God, only to find yourself disillusioned over broken dreams of working in the open harvest field? Maybe there is something you can do right where you are. God's all-important work is not all contained in the highly visible. Much of it is accomplished in the shadows, and only eternity may reveal the impacts made by those on the sidelines feeling unnecessary.

You may say, "There is nothing I can do. I am in a place of obscurity. No one notices me. I certainly can't write like Paul. My time and life are a waste." May I remind you of another thing Paul was doing while held captive? Colossians 1:9 says, "For this cause we also do not cease to pray for you."

If you can't be out on the battlefield preaching and don't have the gift to write, you can pray for those who are doing those things. Your life is not a waste. You are not where you are by accident. God has a plan for your life, just as He did for the Apostle Paul.

You and I did not live during Paul's time on earth. Sadly, there were no tape/CD recorders, MP3 downloads, or DVDs of his preaching to purchase for later observation, so we will never be privileged to see or hear the verbal sermons he delivered to the people. But we have something precious, wrenched from his heart during times of distress, abandonment, imprisonment, while on the sidelines of activity. We have the comfort of picking up our Bibles and reading the inspired Word of God brought forth by his pen. It could not have been easy for him. How did he acquire ink? From where did the parchment come? Did someone have to smuggle it in when they came to visit? Did he peril his life to write while the Roman soldier's back was turned?

Ministry in the shadows is equally as important as an open, visible ministry. A careless, hurtful remark once made me feel hopeless about my future and the direction God was leading our family. I talked about it with Mom, and she encouraged me by saying, "Cheryl, you don't have to be seen to be heard."

God's wisdom and plans are perfect, and the best thing you and I can do is surrender our will to His and do His work—wherever we are with whatever resources we have, then leave the rest to Him.

5

PICKY EATERS

Jesus said, "Blessed are they which do hunger and thirst after righteousness: for they shall be filled." Matthew 5:6

I sat at the table, frustrated, as I urged Zach to eat. He quickly replied, "But, Mama, I don't like meatloaf!" I then launched into my speech, "I can't cook more than one meal at a time. You have to eat what is in front of you. When I was little, I had to eat whatever Mom put on my plate. There are starving children in other parts of the world. They would love to have your meatloaf!" Oh, those over-used phrases we quote to our children because we worry that they aren't eating enough! As usual, my speech didn't work, and I ended up giving his meatloaf to the dogs.

A lot of planning, time, and energy goes into making a meal, and how frustrating it is to come to the table only to find that those we have cooked for do not like what we have prepared. How fulfilling it is to present the product of our hard work to those who are hungry and who enjoy and appreciate our efforts! It fills my heart with joy to watch my family relish every bite, and to see them go back for seconds is the icing on the cake—no pun intended.

It can be frustrating to cook for a picky eater, and it is tiring to keep repeating such phrases as "but this is so good for you" and "just try it" and "please just take a bite to see if you like it." Could this be how our Heavenly Father feels? He sets a bountiful table before us each time we sit down to read His Word or listen to a preached sermon. He goes to great lengths to plan our spiritual meals according to what is necessary for spiritual nutrition, only to find that when we get to the table, we far too often do not like what we see or hear.

Sometimes we do not want to eat what is put before us because the presentation isn't exactly what we had in mind. How many times have I missed an essential spiritual nutrient because I did not like the preacher? Maybe I had noticed somewhere down the line that they were human, and I reasoned away their message by zoning in on the fact that they were flawed and imperfect. Or maybe I just really didn't want to hear that I lack patience, or I need to spend more time in prayer, or I need to be more dedicated.

So, I pushed back my spiritual plate, crossed my arms, and made up my mind that I was not going to "eat," much less digest, what God had so carefully planned for me and what the minister had labored so long to prepare. There are many ways I can reason it away and justify myself. If one excuse or alibi doesn't work, I seem to be quick to come up with another one.

Preachers are human. They are chosen instruments called by God, messengers to bring forth His Word and necessary truths to the people. They are not perfect by any means. They all have different methods of delivering the burden God has given them. But, whether or not we like the minister on a personal level, we will still be held accountable for the truth they put on our spiritual plates.

God sets the table before us, and He loves to see us come to the table hungry. He loves for us to soak up His Word and rake it in, no matter who presents it to us or how He chooses to get the truth across to us. Some of His Word is easier chewed than others. We all love to lap up sermons about God's love for us and how special we are to Him. But, what about when the message He sends is about forgiving those who hurt us, laying aside sin in our lives so we can draw closer to Him, or resigning our will to His to accomplish what He wants to do through our lives?

God will feed us if we are hungry, and it isn't always presented to us in traditional settings such as personal devotions or seated in a pew. In Psalm 78:19, the children of Israel asked, "Can God furnish a table in the wilderness?" It seemed incredible to them, but they found out that He absolutely could! Right there, in the most unlikely place, He fed them and cared for their needs.

God has spoken to me through some very unlikely channels and people through the years, and I have been spiritually fed and nourished in places far removed from church buildings. I have learned to open my mind and heart to listen and recognize when it is Him endeavoring to meet my spiritual needs. God knows where we are deficient, and He faithfully "sets the table before us" filled with all the goodness and bounty Heaven has to offer! All we have to do is eat.

6

MISSING DAD

"Weeping may endure for a night, but joy cometh in the morning." Psalm 30:5

Each year on Dad's birthday, I always tend to think about and miss him a little more than usual. Not that he isn't always a part of my thinking, and not that he doesn't continually occupy a spot in my heart reserved just for him. He is, and he forever will.

Dad was a very humble, unassuming man, and though he never cared much whether or not we made an occasion out of his birthday, Kevin and I always tried to make it extra-special. Dad loved to eat, and we spent many happy birthdays in restaurants he enjoyed.

Dad and Kevin had a special bond. Long before the "redneck" jokes, Dad would often call at suppertime and ask Kevin, "Jeet jet?" Kevin would answer, "No, jou?" (In everyday English, "Did you eat yet?" and "No, did you?"). It was a long-running joke between the two of them, and that is just the way Dad spoke. He was born and raised in Tennessee, and that southern accent followed him all his life.

Dad's home going to Heaven left a vast, gaping hole in all of our hearts. He had suffered from so many physical ailments for so long, and we had become so accustomed to his chronic illnesses that we assumed the last time he entered the hospital would end like all the times before—he would get better and come back home.

One of the most perplexing mysteries of my life is that Dad never got to meet Zach. I will never forget the way Kevin prayed, as he and I knelt side by side right after Dad died. Our hearts were grieving—not only over losing Dad but also that he would not be there when our baby was to be born six months later. I remember how hard I cried as I listened to Kevin asking God to somehow let the spirit of the unborn child He was sending us connect with Dad's spirit that had departed. It may sound like an unusual and far-fetched way to pray—deep grief has a way of producing such prayers. When I observe how much Zach reminds me of Dad, I wonder if maybe God answered that uncommon prayer.

I miss baking a birthday cake for Dad and doing little things for him. I know he is enjoying eternal bliss far beyond anything I could ever do for him, and the treasures of Heaven far outweigh any earthly joy. I know he would not come back if God gave him the choice, and he is in a place where there is no more pain. If he could send me a message, I think he would tell me not to grieve. I can just hear him urging me to stay true to God and to be faithful because he surely would not want me to miss what he is enjoying right now.

I can only imagine his face when he first saw Heaven. One time, he flew from where we lived in Florida to his home state of Tennessee to attend a funeral. I remember how enthralled and excited he was when he called to tell me about the flight. He kept saying how I wouldn't believe it and "it was just gigantic!" Imagine how he felt when he first saw what God has prepared for those who love Him!

I don't know all of the ins and outs about where we immediately go when we die in the Lord. All of the theories I have heard have this one thing in common—believers who die go to a place of rest, and on that final Judgment day, Heaven will be their eternal home. It gives me great comfort to know that Dad is resting, that he doesn't hurt anymore, the deep worry lines on his face have all been erased, and he is safe with Jesus.

I wish I could sing "Happy Birthday" to him, just one more time, but Lord willing, one day, we will all sing together with a choir of angels around the throne of God! I guess I would never bring him back to this sin-benighted world, even if I had the power. It would be a most selfish thing to do when I consider the troubled life he had to live. If anyone ever deserved Heaven, it was Dad. I miss him terribly, but I am so thankful to know Jesus is looking out for him now. If he were still alive, he would be nearing 90 years old. What comfort it brings that he is now in a place where he will never grow old!

7
IN HIS IMAGE

"So, God created man in His image...male and female created He them." Genesis 1:27

I stood on the scales, dreading to make eye contact with the glaring digital numbers staring up at me. I had tried so hard and deprived myself and purposely made wise choices, but was it enough? I summoned the courage to look—slowly, I peered at the number. Exactly eight ounces! My heart sank, and my whole day took a decidedly negative plunge. Why couldn't I lose weight? What more could I do to make it happen? I began to scold myself and feel very worthless as self-berating thoughts swirled around in my head. It wasn't long until the Lord began to deal with me, and I began to feel sorry for the self-deprecation I was inflicting.

Should numbers on a scale define who I am? Should seeing them determine whether I am going to have a good or bad day? In the grand scheme of life and eternity, is it all that important?

I feel guilt over allowing myself to gain the amount of weight I have gained. I am very aware that I should take better care of the temple in which God's Spirit dwells, and this is an area in which I desperately need more self-control. But it occurs to me that who I am—*the real me* is dearly cherished by my Creator, despite all. He doesn't look at my outward appearance. He looks at my heart. I Samuel 16:7 says, "...for man looketh on the outward appearance, but the Lord looketh on the heart." My obesity does not alter the fact that He loves me—unconditionally—no matter what.

My thoughts turn, as they so often do, to Zachary. I am so glad God chose to allow me to assist Him in the miracle process of creating a new life! How hurtful it is to hear him put himself down and make degrading remarks when his performance is less than he knows it could have been! It hurts because I am his mother, and he is a part and an extension of me.

How it must hurt and grieve our Heavenly Father when we degrade ourselves, and we despise the physical bodies He so carefully designed! Psalm 139:14 says, "I will praise Thee; for I am fearfully and wonderfully made." Instead of focusing on the outside flaws and imperfections and areas that need improvement, I need to praise Him for the healthy body He has given and all the incredible blessings He has bestowed.

II Corinthians 10:12 tells us that "comparing ourselves among ourselves is not wise." When I compare myself to those around me who are thinner, prettier, or even more spiritual, I am using an unwise and man-made gauge that is not used or even recognized by the One who made me. Society places unrealistic demands and generates pressure on us to conform to earthly "images." This takes our focus off the actual image we are created in and are endeavoring to emulate.

So, I will continue to try hard to lose this excess weight. I will do the things I know I need to do—drink more water, exercise more often, and continue making healthier eating choices. I will remind myself that God is more concerned with how closely I conform to His image than with external, fleshly standards. And I will try to remember that even when I mess up and fall short, He loves me just the same, and nothing about me will ever change that.

8

MORE GRACE

"But He giveth more grace." James 4:6

I knew the minute she walked in the bank door, she was not a typical, run-of-the-mill customer, and soon after she sat down at my desk, I realized I was going to need "more grace." The average amount it took to get through a day in my job as a Customer Service Representative was not going to be enough. I took a deep breath and braced myself, just wanting the transaction to be over.

One of the aspects of our training taught us that people have one of four predominant personality types. The *driver* is the strong, bossy one who takes command and expects everyone else to follow. The *promoter* is the energetic, optimistic type whose enthusiasm alone enables them to sell just about anything. The *socializer* is the outgoing, friendly, social butterfly who flitters incessantly, rarely lighting on their workspace and accomplishing little. Lastly, there is the **thinker**— the serious, studious, diligent type who loves details and never decides on impulse.

I figured out quickly that the lady seated at my desk could have been the **driver** poster girl. She continually bossed her poor husband to do this and do that, barking orders like a drill sergeant. Evidently, he was used to it, judging by the way he so quickly complied to her every whim. It occurred to me that he had probably learned long ago that he would never win an argument, so he should cooperate.

We settled into the transaction, and it turned out that this couple was far from being financially deprived. The amount of the check she tossed onto my desk was equal to about five years of my annual salary! I began to make suggestions based on what I thought would be their best investment opportunity, but she quickly found something to argue about no matter what recommendation I made. Nothing pleased her. She fussed and fumed and complained over pretty much everything I said. I knew what was on the line—this was a lot of money, and it was my job not to let it walk out the door.

Internally fighting impatience and frustration over the apparent impossibility of pleasing this woman, I had just about reached the end of tolerating her belligerent behavior, and I knew I desperately needed help from the Lord. There was no way I could discreetly leave my desk to find an alone spot to pray, so imagine my surprise when I suddenly felt an inward shift! God sent the answer to my unspoken cry for "more grace" without me even needing to ask!

As that extra boost of grace took over, I turned to look at the miserable woman seated across from me, this time trying hard to see her through Jesus' eyes. I listened and gave validation to her complaining. The wonderful infusion of a greater portion of grace eased the tension, and she ended up opening the account and leaving as close to happy as I believe this sad woman was capable.

That challenging transaction began a long-standing banking relationship, and as time went on, I saw her often. Each time, she complained and was extremely hard to deal with, but for some reason, she began to trust me and even got to the point where she would call me just to talk. My co-workers found her intolerable, but through God's grace alone, I listened and empathized with her. As she confided in me, I discovered that she was bitter over her dream of having children never becoming a reality. She had been hurt and mistreated and abused. The wounds had turned her into someone who continually did the same hurtful things to others.

God kept giving "more grace," and over time, we became friends. She invited Kevin and me to her home for pumpkin pie and coffee, and at another time, she and her husband went out to dinner with us. There came a day when I was transferred to another branch, and slowly, I began to hear from her less and less. One day, I heard that she had gone into a restaurant, fallen suddenly to the floor, and died instantly.

Memories flooded my mind of the first time I met her up until I stopped hearing from her. It was then I realized God's grace is sufficient in every circumstance, with every person, no matter how difficult they may be or how long-standing the relationship. II Corinthians 12:9 says, "And He said unto me, 'My grace is sufficient for thee: for My strength is made perfect in weakness.' Most gladly, therefore, will I rather glory in my infirmities, that the power of Christ may rest upon me." God placed a test in front of me with this customer, and He wanted me to go the extra mile to prove the sufficiency of His grace. It was a challenge I was incapable of rising to on my own, but the grace of God did what I could never do.

Do you know someone who requires "more grace?" God's well of grace never runs dry. It will enable you to be kind, no matter how you are being treated. We never know how long we will have to "put up with" a difficult person, but no matter how long they are in our life, God's grace will be there. When you feel you have reached the end of your endurance and you are ready to quit, remember God still has "more grace." No matter how much grace you have used up, He will always have more, and He always gives it when we need it most.

9

THE LAST QUAIL

> *"Let this mind be in you, which was also in Christ Jesus: Who, being in the form of God, thought it not robbery to be equal with God: but made Himself of no reputation, and took upon Him the form of a servant, and was made in the likeness of men: and being found in fashion as a man, He humbled Himself, and became obedient unto death, even the death of the cross." Philippians 2:5-8*

*H*ave you ever felt walked on, that your opinions do not count, and it doesn't matter to others how they are treating you? While going through such an experience, I found myself entirely disregarded by the ones around me. The leadership position I held commanded respect that was not being shown, and I felt like I should stand up for myself and stop letting people treat me as if I were invisible.

One day as Zach and I were homeschooling, our lesson was

about the pecking order of quails. The top quail can peck all of the other quails, but none of them are allowed to peck back. The second quail in the pecking order can peck everyone except the first quail. The third quail can peck everyone except the first two. The pattern continues until the last quail—it can be pecked by all of the other quails, yet it cannot peck back—no matter what.

The familiar, still, small voice of the precious Holy Spirit whispered, "Child, that is you. You are the last quail." My instant reaction was, "But, Lord! That isn't fair! They are not treating me right or respecting my position." I went on and on laying out all the reasons I didn't deserve what I was going through, reminding Him how hard I was working, how much I was sacrificing, and trying to convince our all-wise, all-knowing Heavenly Father to see my point of view.

After I had ranted for quite a while, He gently reminded me of the cross— of Jesus hanging there, though He didn't have to—of the self-sacrificing life He lived so that I could have this great salvation. The Son of God, Creator of the universe, Lord of lords, and King of kings **made Himself** of **no reputation** and willfully laid down His rights to defend Himself. He was in Heaven, living in a perfect world, at one with His Father, and had every right to stay there and empathize with humankind from a distance. But He chose to leave Heaven, come down, and make Himself of *no reputation.* He laid it all down, took upon Him the form of a servant, and lowered Himself to the lowest station in life—*intentionally.*

I felt so ashamed. How could anything I ever go through compare even in the slightest degree with what He suffered for me? When the abusers were inflicting their injustices, He didn't cry out, "What do you think you're doing? Do you know Who I am? You have no right to hurt Me. I created you. I should not be serving you—you should be serving Me! The sins I am so severely punished for are your sins, not Mine." The Bible says He answered not a word. No retaliation. No pecking back. He was a servant to all humanity—by choice.

Jesus, who was and is equal with God, became obedient and laid down His rights at the foot of that old, rugged cross. That day, as He dealt with me, I realized that is precisely what I must do, too, and as I did, the raging war within me ceased. Consecration and total surrender to His will always produce the same results of perfect soul rest and peace. Jesus overcame all by submission to His Father's will, and He is now seated in Heaven at the right hand of His Father. One day, by His grace and by following the same path He did, I hope to be there, too.

10

TWENTY-ONE DAYS

"Then he said unto me, Fear not, Daniel: for from the first day that thou didst set thine heart to understand...thy words were heard." Daniel 10:12

*I*t had been an exceptionally long 21 days for Mom and all of us. At 83 years old, she had undergone emergency surgery, then had to spend three weeks in the hospital, and we were all utterly exhausted. When the Lord answered our prayers, and Mom was well enough to come home on the 21st day, I was reminded of the story recorded in Daniel chapter 10.

For 21 long days, no matter how hard he prayed, Daniel received no answer from God. Finally, on the 21st day, an angel came to him and said, "Fear not, Daniel: for ***from the first day*** that thou didst set thine heart to understand and to chasten thyself before thy God, thy words were heard, and I am come for thy words. But the prince of the kingdom of Persia withstood me one and twenty days: but, lo, Michael, one of the chief princes, came to help me, and I remained there with the kings of Persia."

Daniel was faithful to keep praying for three whole weeks, even though he saw no outward evidence that his prayers were even being heard. Imagine the comfort he must have felt to hear that even though there had been no proof that God was listening or working behind the scenes, the truth was God had heard his prayer **the very first day!**

I believe this was true in Mom's situation. Though we had been praying for 21 days for God to heal her and allow her to come back home, there had been no guarantee that would ever happen. When the surgeon came to talk to us that first night in the Emergency Room, her situation was grim. I remember the fear that welled inside as he told us they could not postpone doing surgery until morning. "Do you mean you are going to do it tonight?" I asked. "I mean now!" was his firm response.

A few years prior, Mom had undergone another operation. The surgeon had told us that Mom's body could never withstand another bout of anesthesia due to her age and condition. As I finished relaying this information to the surgeon standing in front of me, he said, "You're praying, aren't you?" "Yes!" I quickly replied. He said, "Well, it's all gonna be all right then."

How he knew I was praying, I do not know. I got the feeling he was a Christian and that he knew the outcome was never in his hands.

There is a beginning and an end to every trial we go through. Sometimes, they are 21 days long—sometimes shorter, many times longer. Regardless of the length of our battles, Jesus is the Author and the Finisher of our faith—in every trial and situation. (Hebrews 12:2) He doesn't walk away when we enter into a trial and leave us to suffer alone. He walks with us, stays by our side the whole time, then walks us out on the other side, no matter how long it takes.

Seeing Mom come into her little apartment on that 21st day was a modern-day, divine miracle. It reinforced my faith and reminded me that I serve the same God Daniel served. God does not show favoritism; He does not love one of His children more than another. "For there is no respect of persons with God." Romans 2:11 The main thing He is looking for in us is faith and persistence like Daniel had to keep praying, even when it seems that nothing is happening, and we question if we are even being heard.

Do you have a burden on your heart? Does it seem the night will never end? Have you prayed for a long time, only to feel that the heavens are brass? I want to assure you that God heard your cry the very first time you prayed and every time after that. He is always listening. He never sleeps, and just because you haven't yet seen the answer to your prayers does not mean He is not working on your problem. Keep praying and knocking on Heaven's door. Who knows, today could be your "21st day!"

11

STORMS IN THE NIGHT

"This poor man cried, and the Lord heard him and saved him out of all his troubles." Psalm 34:6

When Kevin was working the late-night shift, I awoke one morning around 4:00 am, startled to realize he was not home from work. I called his cell phone, and when he answered, I could hear a horrendous storm raging on the other end. He described limbs of trees strewn about in the road, I could hear a transformer exploding near him, and the torrential rain prevented him from driving more than about 25 miles per hour.

Needless to say, I hit my knees and cried out to God to protect and bring him home safe. I began to question why God had let the storm come while Kevin was driving home in the dark. Why couldn't it have waited until he was safely home? Immediately, I felt the comfort of the Holy Spirit assuring me that the reason He allowed it to happen while Kevin was on the road was two-fold. He wanted to prove to me that He was able to bring him home safe *through the worst possible physical storm* and to show me that He can carry His children *through the worst possible storms of life.*

A short time later, the storm reached our house, rain began to fall, and I watched through our open front door as tree branches swayed in the ever-increasing wind. Under normal circumstances, I would have been afraid, but I knew God was proving His faithfulness to me, and I needed to trust Him to keep His word. Soon, I saw our car's headlights shining in the driveway. Kevin was home —a bit rattled but safe and sound through God's providential care —just as He had assured me only moments before.

Mark 4:35-41 tells the story of when Jesus was in a boat with His disciples and told them to cross to the other side of the lake. As they rowed, He fell asleep, and while He was sleeping, a tremendous stormy wind arose and began to violently toss the ship. Jesus' disciples became terrified, woke Him, and said, "Master, carest thou not that we perish?' And He arose, and rebuked the wind, and said unto the sea, 'Peace, be still.' And the wind ceased, and there was a great calm."

Of course, Jesus cared if they perished! But the fact that He was asleep on a pillow in the back of the boat made them feel that He was either not aware of their situation or that He wasn't concerned about what they were going through. While walking through the storms of life, I must admit that I, too, have wondered if Jesus was sleeping through the storm and found myself asking the same type of questions. Lord, are You there? Are You still with me? Do You care that I am going under?

All along, Jesus was in complete control of the disciples' circumstances. And even though He could have postponed the storm until they were safe on land, He chose to allow it to happen while they were in the most peril to prove His power to deliver *in*

even the worst circumstances. God could have held off the storm until Kevin was safe at home, but He wanted to prove the same lesson to me that stormy night.

He doesn't always remove storms from our path; sometimes, He requires us to weather them. He doesn't always postpone their onset until we feel safe and in pleasant circumstances; sometimes, the full force of a trial comes at what feels like the most inopportune time. But, no matter when we face a storm or how inconvenient the timing, Jesus always remains "in the boat" with us, and having Him continually onboard changes everything.

12

SUPERHEROES

"And he said, thy name shall be called no more Jacob, but Israel: for as a prince has thou power with God and with men, and hast prevailed." Genesis 32:28

Zach has always loved superheroes, and he has also always had quite an imagination. Since he was a little boy, he has loved buying action figures, and I have enjoyed listening to his imaginary battles with them. Sometimes, the fighting has sounded pretty intense, and I have wondered who would win—the superhero or the villain? Ultimately, the good guy always ended up winning, destroying the bad guy in the process—after all, Zach could control the outcome, so the result could be whatever he wanted it to be.

Come to find out, each of these fictional superheroes has its particular areas of strength and power, and there is a story behind how they were acquired. Some have even gone through transformations and received new names after becoming who they are now, and Zach has always enjoyed telling me their backstories. While listening, my mind drifts off to real-life superheroes I know and have known—those I consider to be spiritual giants who have encouraged me in my walk with Christ and those I admire and look up to as living much closer to God than I do. When observing my spiritual superheroes, I see courage, spiritual maturity, and stalwart faith. I see them as they are today, but I fail to consider how they got to where they are, what it cost them, and what they have gone through to attain such strength and power with God.

When Jacob wrestled all night with the angel, he made up his mind that he would not let go until he received the blessing and spiritual "power" he was seeking. The battle was intense and long-lasting, but just before daybreak, his persistence was rewarded when told, "as a prince hast thou power with God and with men, and hast prevailed." In that pivotal moment, his life was forever changed, and to mark his inner transformation, the angel gave Jacob a new name—the name of Israel. It is vital to notice the distinct difference in the meaning of the two names—Jacob means "supplanter" or "deceiver," which was appropriate to his deceptive nature in the past, and Israel, means "a prince of God," which foretells his role and position in the founding of the future nation of Israel. Jacob was changed! Old things had passed away; behold, all things had become new. (II Corinthians 5:17)

Every spiritual superhero has a backstory—a time of past life lived in a sinful state, a time of wrestling with God and truth, and a moment of transformation that marks their transition from darkness to light.

In G.M. Day's book, "Wonder of the Word," we find a glimpse into one such backstory, that of the 4th-century spiritual giant, Augustine. "Shortly after his new birth experience, Augustine met a prostitute on the street. Pretending not to see her, he attempted to pass by without recognition, but she called, "Augustine, it is I." He turned to her then and answered, "Yes, but it is not I."

In times of discouragement, inadequacy, and failure, it is good to remind ourselves that our spiritual superheroes weren't always the champions we look up to and admire. Each waged their battles against the archenemy of all souls—this "villain" with whom we are all constantly at war. And while we can look up to them and want what they have, we will never reach the spiritual depths they have attained by sitting on the sidelines, envying their close relationship with Jesus. We must be willing to put on the whole armor of God, get in the fight, and win our own battles against the enemy.

Many who have extensively impacted my walk with the Lord have already won their ultimate "boss" battle and scored an eternal victory. I look back on the ones I have studied and known through childhood and up until today, and I thank God for allowing them to be a part of my journey. They have influenced me to dig deep and inspired a longing to be more like Christ. I love to read and hear about them and wish I could ask them all how they got to where they are and allow them to show me their battle scars.

Do we aspire to be spiritual superheroes—one of those giants in the faith? Are we willing to lose a night's sleep to "wrestle" with God in prayer to get what we crave and are seeking from Him? How badly do we want it? The school of hard knocks is not an easy instructor, but as I ponder some of my spiritual superheroes and realize how much I admire them and the power they have attained with God, I conclude that it is worth whatever He requires.

13

BROKEN HEARTS

> *"The Spirit of the Lord God is upon Me; because the Lord hath anointed Me to preach good tidings unto the meek; He hath sent Me to bind up the brokenhearted, to proclaim liberty to the captives, and the opening of the prison to them that are bound." Isaiah 61:1*

As I sat in the hospital emergency room waiting for the staff to return with Mom from the radiology department, I thought about how remarkable it is that medical diagnostic machines can see inside every internal organ of the human body. Who could have dreamed that there would come a day when modern technology would enable the trained eyes of medical professionals to peer through layers of skin, muscles, tendons, and ligaments, right down to the bones inside a person! But regardless of how much science has progressed, there is still a part of humanity that will never show up on an X-ray, CT scan, PET scan, MRI, or ultrasound. It will never be seen by the eyes of even the most skillfully trained physician or discovered by the most brilliant diagnostic machine. Doctors can speculate and even prescribe something to treat and mask the symptoms, but sitting there in that crowded place, I knew something was going on in the deepest part of me that they could never see—I had a broken heart.

There is only One who could see, only One who could diagnose, and only One who could heal what was wrong with me. Jesus sees through every layer—not just the physical parts of these mortal bodies that will one day return to dust, but even crushed feelings, torn emotional "muscles," and inflicted hurts. He sees all the way to the inside of the most broken places in the human heart. How reassuring to know that there are some things He still reserves to Himself—that only He can do with His Own nail-scarred hands!

When I was young, I thought there was no one in the world like my brother-in-law, Bruce. He was incredibly kind and always took the time to make me feel special. Once, during a family picnic at the park, I wandered off alone on my bike, ended up going way too fast down a hill, flipped over the handlebars, and landed in the ditch. I was terrified and shaking as I walked my bike up the hill to where my family was gathered. Bruce was the first to notice, and I will never forget how he rushed to my rescue, sat me down at the picnic table, and assessed my injuries. It didn't take him long to figure out I had a severely sprained wrist – the injury was external and easy to see and diagnose. In a few weeks, the sprain had healed, and all that remained was a scar. The hurt that enveloped my little, broken heart several months later when Bruce and my sister stopped by our home to tell us they were ending their marriage in divorce was quite another story.

Isaiah 61:1-3 is a prophecy of Jesus Christ and gives the whole reason the Messiah was sent to earth from Heaven. In verse one, we read, "The Spirit of the Lord GOD *is* upon Me; because the LORD hath anointed Me to preach good tidings unto the meek; **He hath sent Me to bind up the brokenhearted.**"

Jesus understands better than anyone else how it feels to have a broken heart. Hebrews 4:15 says, "For we have not an high priest which cannot be touched with the feeling of our infirmities; but was in all points tempted like as *we are, yet* without sin." His cry of "My God! My God! Why hast Thou forsaken Me?" was not because of the gaping wounds that resulted from the brutal Roman scourging. It wasn't because each time He tried to inhale, His torn and mutilated back raked across sharp fragments on the old, rugged cross. It wasn't because He could not wipe the blood from His eyes as it dripped from the thorn crown pressed into His skull. Jesus' anguished cry from the cross was because, in those excruciating moments of agony and feelings of being God-forsaken, His heart was broken.

His very purpose for coming into this hurting world was to heal brokenness, such as I felt realizing Bruce would no longer be a part of our family and again that night with Mom in the emergency room. *He came to receive a broken heart so He could heal our hearts when they break.* Jesus intentionally and voluntarily suffered this intense level of brokenness to feel what we feel and endure our pain. How can we even measure that kind of love? It goes beyond any love man has ever known. "Greater love hath no man than this, that a man lay down his life for his friends." John 15:13

Do you have a broken heart? Do you cry in silence, feeling no one sees or even cares? Have you tried to explain, only to find that no one understands? Hope can still be found in the one person who loves you so much that He was willing to go through what you are going through to prove that love. He didn't promise our hearts would never break, but He promised to bind them when they do.

14

ELANORE

"A man that hath friends must shew himself friendly."
    Proverbs 18:24

When I was 17, I worked in a flower shop near Vanderbilt Beach in Naples, Florida. One evening near closing time, I heard the familiar bell of the front door ring and looked up to see a well-dressed older lady coming in. From the moment I saw her, it was plain to see that she was distinguished and well-to-do. As our eyes met, she said, "Come outside! You have to see this!"

I came from around the counter at the back of the store and walked with her to the sidewalk outside. There we stood, two strangers side-by-side, gazing at one of the most beautiful sunsets I had ever seen. When the moment was over, she followed me back into the store and began to open her heart. I could tell she was very lonely and longing for someone to listen—so I did. She told me her name was Elanore (spelled just this way), she sorely missed her deceased husband, Eddie, and even though he had been gone for about six years, she was still struggling to adjust to life without him.

As time went by, Elanore would come by the shop when she needed to talk. Through our chats, I came to feel that I knew Eddie and found that he had cared deeply for Elanore and made sure she would be financially comfortable after his death. She loved to tell me the story of how he had bought the land she lived on near Vanderbilt Beach for $32,000 many years before. At the time I met her, it was worth well over a million dollars.

Soon, she began to invite me to her home for visits, and we developed a dear friendship that would span the next 25 years. It wasn't long before I realized I needed Elanore as much as she needed me. Things at home were shaky and unsettled, and Elanore's care and concern about the things I was going through brought a deep sense of comfort.

I distinctly remember a time I was struggling hard to help Mom and Dad make ends meet, and I was not going to be able to pay a car payment that was coming due. It crossed my mind to call my dear friend and ask if she would consider helping me out, but I was so conflicted inside and worried that she would think I was trying to take advantage of her or overstep boundaries to ask such a thing. Being independent and never wanting to put anyone out, it just did not feel like the right thing to do. Still, I found myself situated between a rock and a hard place, and desperation finally drove me to dial her number. She answered the phone, and I nervously and apologetically asked her if I could borrow $150. It sounded like such a large amount of money to me, and I felt so ashamed! Without the slightest hesitation, Elanore graciously made arrangements to loan me the money. When I got there, she handed me an envelope, I thanked her profusely, and we parted ways. Imagine my surprise when I got into my car and opened the envelope to find $300! Her generosity and the trust she placed in me made me determined to live the kind of life that would merit that trust.

Elanore never asked me to sign a promissory note and didn't even want me to make regular payments. She said I could just pay her as I had extra money. One day I went to her house to drop off a payment, and I will never forget what she said when I got there. "Cheryl, you don't need to repay anymore of the money. All I ask is that someday, down the line, you help another young girl who needs help." If I remember right, I believe I still owed her about $150.

One day, Elanore came by the shop with a sparkle in her eyes that I had never seen before. She couldn't wait to tell me that she had met a nice gentleman, and they were getting married! Soon, I met Howard, her new beau, and I found him a true gem.

A few years later, I moved away, met Kevin, and we fell in love. On our wedding day, Elanore and Howard were there—so happy, simply because I was happy. Kevin and I settled into our life together, and when I missed Elanore, I would give her a call. It made me feel special when Howard would answer, hear it was me, then say, "Elanore! Pick up the phone! It's Cheryl!" I could hear her say, "Oh!" and shuffle towards the phone as quickly as she could.

I'll never forget the last time I saw her. Zach was just a baby, and we made it a point to make sure she and Howard got to meet him while we were in town visiting relatives. It shocked me to see how frail she had become. I hated leaving her that day. I knew in my heart I was seeing her for the last time.

I continued to call her after we got home. Her hearing deteriorated to the point that she could barely hear my voice, but still, I would call. One day, almost six years after the last time I saw her, I called, and her daughter told me she was gone. My tears fell like rain.

We must have seemed like an unlikely pair when we became friends—she an energetic, spunky, financially secure 69-year-old, and me an insecure, struggling 17-year-old, but God knew how much we needed each other. I am glad I took the time one day to send a card telling her how much she meant to me and how much I appreciated her and our precious friendship.

I learned so much from Elanore, and I still find myself hearing her advice when I hear of someone in need. She taught me to give without ever wanting to be paid back.

15

FOGGY CONDITIONS

"And they were in the way going up to Jerusalem, and Jesus went before them." Mark 10:32

The early morning fog was thick as we wound our way through the mountains. I was driving, and at times, I could not see two feet in front of the car. Kevin and I talked about how it looked like a good morning to see deer out and about, so I was trying to be extra careful. During the particularly dense spots, there was one thing that kept me moving forward—there was a car ahead of us, and my eyes stayed fixed on its lights. If there were obstacles, the vehicle in front of us would encounter them and tackle them first.

As I drove along, I thought of the perplexing set of circumstances through which we were walking. God had led us to walk away from what we knew as familiar, and in the aftermath, we found ourselves in a fog of uncertainty. We knew we had minded God to that point but had no idea where our next step would take us, nor could we see anything ahead very clearly. One thing gave us the courage to walk forward in faith through the fog—we were following the Light. Jesus said in John 8:12, "I am the Light of the world: he that followeth Me shall not walk in darkness but shall have the light of life." Just as Jesus went *before* His disciples as they walked to Jerusalem, He was walking in front of us, and we took comfort in knowing whatever was out there, He would confront and deal with it first.

I don't suppose there is any greater fear than the fear of the unknown. We all experience it, and Jesus understands. Without the light of His presence, we would find ourselves completely immobilized, unable to move forward. But, knowing He goes before us, and nothing touches us that doesn't touch Him first brings about a peace that passes all human understanding. (Philippians 4:7)

I always want to see the big picture. I want to know why? And how long? And what's next? But any one of us who has followed Jesus for any length of time can attest that the Christian walk is often traveled in foggy conditions. 2 Corinthians 5:7 says, "For we walk by faith, not by sight." If we could see far ahead of us, why would we need faith? When the future direction of our lives is foggy and uncertain, how relieving it is to know that we are not in the lead, stumbling along in the dark! The precious Lamb of God goes directly in front of us, and we are following His light.

What about you? Have things been predictable for years, and do you suddenly find yourself in strange, unfamiliar territory and circumstances? Is everything foggy ahead, unclear, and uncertain? Are you afraid of what's going to happen next? Maybe you are awaiting the results of a medical test for you or a loved one. Perhaps you don't know where the next mortgage payment is coming from or how you will continue to feed your family. Whatever is out there, the light of Jesus' presence goes before you. Nothing that is happening in your life has come as a surprise to Him. He already knows the future, and He is prepared and capable of handling it with you. Hebrews 13:5 says, "...for He hath said, I will never leave thee, nor forsake thee."

It has now been many years since that foggy mountain morning. The future so mysterious and frightening to us then is now a part of our distant past. I rejoice in telling you that the fog eventually lifted, God has continually been faithful, and the Light has never gone out.

16

SPARROWS

"Fear ye not, therefore, ye are of more value than many sparrows." Matthew 10:31

As I walked through the room, I heard Zach and his cousin having a conversation about birds. It had started snowing the evening before, continued snowing all through the night, and left behind a beautiful, soft, white blanket on the ground outside. Earlier, we had gone out and built a snowman, then come back inside to get warm. Now the two boys were raring to get back outside—this time to look for birds. I heard them mention sparrows.

    Always eager for an opportunity to insert some valuable spiritual lesson, I stopped what I was doing and said, "Do you know God sees every time a sparrow falls to the ground? He cares **that much** about sparrows. And Jesus said **you** are worth more than many sparrows. So, if God cares that much about a little, tiny sparrow and you are worth more than many of them, just imagine how much He loves you! Don't ever forget!" After they promised they wouldn't, I felt satisfied that I had gotten my point across and left them to their outdoor plans.

As I walked away, I wondered how many times I have heard every one of those statements throughout life. Growing up in a Christian home, regularly going to church, and attending Christian schools that used a Bible-saturated curriculum gave me the advantage of hearing them more times than I can even remember. I wonder if we've all heard them so often that they have become commonplace, and we no longer grasp the depth of their meaning?

We live in an age of time that the Gospel of Jesus Christ is widely proclaimed. Radio, television, and the internet have provided many mediums to hear the old, old story of Jesus and His love. We often hear, "God loves you. Jesus died for you. He rose from the dead on the third day. He went away to prepare a beautiful place for you. One day soon, He is coming again to take His children home to live with Him for eternity." Could hearing these statements so often have made us become what we refer to as "Gospel-hardened" until the effect of the Word has lost its impact? Do we believe it when we hear "God loves you" anymore?

As I consider my struggles with feelings of worthlessness, I realize that my opinion and God's opinion of me are worlds apart. I measure my love-worthiness by my failures, the times I have fallen short, and the many times I have let Him down. He measures my worth by a completely different standard. Romans 8:35-39 names no less than 17 things that threaten to cause God to stop loving us. It encompasses every possible element in this life, and then it assures us that none of them "shall be able to separate us from the love of God which is in Christ Jesus our Lord." (verse 39)

Perhaps our backgrounds are different, and maybe you haven't heard the words "God loves you" as often as I have. Whether the meaning has diminished by hearing them often or you haven't heard them often enough, one fact remains—God loves you. It doesn't matter who you are, where you are, what you have done, or how far below God's standards of holiness you are living—you are worth more to Him than many sparrows. Your current condition does not alter the amount of love He poured out when He sent His Son to die for you. Jesus knew where you would be *today* when He hung on the cruel cross. It did not deter him from His mission of demonstrating the depths of His love for you. Contrariwise, it compelled and made Him want to die for you all the more because He knew you would need a Savior. Nothing you have done or will ever do will alter the fact that He loves you. ***Don't ever forget.***

17

A GOOD NAME

"A good name is rather to be chosen than great riches."
Proverbs 22:1

When I was growing up and would leave my parents to go off with a friend or to spend the night with someone, Dad always offered me the same parting piece of advice. "Always remember, Cheryl. Whatever you do, however you act, is a direct reflection on your Mom and me." I lost count of the times that fatherly admonition and reminder kept me on the straight and narrow because I did not want to make Mom and Dad look bad. Knowing my behavior reflected on them directly made me stop and think before I acted because I wanted others to see them as the good and caring people they were.

Kevin's Dad's last name was important to him, also. He always taught Kevin to cherish and keep it reputable by the life he lives each day. He took pleasure in knowing Kevin is carrying on his name as his son, and Zach is doing the same as his grandson.

Through the years, I heard him mention many times, with pride, that Zach will now carry on the "Smith" name through another generation. Smith is an overwhelmingly common name, but he was most concerned about *his* bloodline and legacy.

Both of our earthly fathers instilled caution in Kevin and me about how we present their "name" to the world around us. Then one day, we were both adopted into another family—the family of God. Jesus paid a great price for our adoption, and we took on a new name—the name of Christian. Just as our earthy fathers valued their family names, God, our Heavenly Father, has a deep interest in how His name is represented to the world. Every act, word, tone of voice, and mannerism presents Christianity negatively or positively.

Mom always told me that watching a Christian life is the only Bible some people will ever read. What a responsibility that places upon us, as Christians! If someone in our life is "reading the Bible" solely by watching how we live, what are they reading? How is the name of Christ being presented to the world around us when we tell them we are a "Christian?"

One day, Zach and I went into a health store, and I needed assistance from the clerk. I could see right away that her personality was unpleasant. It was one of those situations where you wish you could avoid the salesperson altogether, but Mom was elderly and waiting for us in the car, and I needed help in finding something quickly. When I got to the counter to complete the transaction, the price was far more than I thought it should have been, and when I asked her about it, she became defensive and started raising her voice. Before I realized it, I responded in the same way while trying to get my point across. Thankfully, she, Zach, and I were the only ones in the store, but it hurts to think *he* saw me react the way I did. While we aren't responsible for, nor can we control, the actions of those around us, we *are* accountable for *our reactions* to what they do and say.

All at once, I realized I was not reflecting a positive light on who Jesus is, and I felt so ashamed. I stopped what I was doing, looked her square in the eye, and said, "Ma'am, I am so sorry. I am a Christian, and I did not mean to talk to you the way I just did. Please forgive me." Completely caught off guard, her attitude changed, and she calmly explained the price to me. I finally understood what she had been trying to tell me and left the store with a mixture of feeling ashamed over my behavior and humbled by having needed to apologize.

When we got outside, I told Zach how sorry I was and begged his forgiveness. My behavior made my family look bad, and more importantly, it made Jesus look bad. It didn't matter that "she started it" or that I was simply trying to defend my position. What mattered is that I didn't react to her actions in the right tone of voice or in a Christlike way. It is weighty to realize that people expect us to be and act like Him when we profess His name.

We all face moments of weakness, times we aren't feeling well, or situations in which someone rubs us the wrong way. I'm so thankful that even though God places great value on His name and how we represent Him, He is also merciful and quick to forgive when we fall short of His expectations.

18

WINDOWS OF OPPORTUNITY

> *"And He was teaching in one of the synagogues on the Sabbath. And behold, there was a woman which had a spirit of infirmity eighteen years, and was bowed together, and could in no wise lift up herself. And when Jesus saw her, He called her to Him and said unto her, 'Woman, thou art loosed from thine infirmity.' And He laid His hands on her: and immediately she was made straight, and glorified God." Luke 13:10-13*

*J*love this story. It is not one of the more widely proclaimed miracles Jesus performed, and the actual event takes up only four little verses in the book of Luke, but it speaks volumes about the character of our Lord.

While teaching in the synagogue, Jesus spotted a woman in the crowd whose physical frame was grossly disfigured and had been that way for 18 years. As a great sense of compassion rose within Him over her condition, He turned His attention from speaking to the crowd *to speaking only to her.* Jesus had a way of making every single person feel that they were the most important person in the world to Him—because they were. This unnamed woman's need surpassed everything else at that moment.

He could have kept teaching and ignored her. The synagogue was more than likely packed with "important" people highly interested in what He had to say. Wouldn't it break tradition for Jesus to disappoint them by an interruption? What would it hurt to wait until the sermon was over? After all, the woman had accepted her condition. There is no indication in this story to lead us to believe she made any effort to ask Jesus for healing. She was just a face in the crowd.

But was she? "When Jesus saw her, He called her to Him." Right then and there—as if she were the only person in the room. I can just imagine the effort behind her lumbered steps as she worked her way to where He was. When she reached Jesus, He spoke words that would forever change her life, "Woman, thou art loosed from thine infirmity." Then Jesus laid His hands on her.

With a few words and a single touch, Jesus changed her whole world. Bent over and unable to lift herself or stand upright for 18 years, how amazed she must have felt to be able to glance around and look the crowd in the eye!

What if Jesus had put His teaching ahead of her need? The woman may have slipped out early to avoid curious glares, and the chance to connect been lost forever. Perhaps their paths would never have crossed again, and she would have continued in misery the rest of her life after coming so close to the healing power of God.

The overwhelming sense of compassion that compelled Jesus to interrupt His sermon to meet her need demonstrates that there is more to the Gospel than staying on schedule or coming under bondage to religious protocol. He was aware of and seized upon every divinely appointed window of opportunity that opened to Him. Nothing was more important to Him than meeting her need.

There are windows of opportunity that open to each of us to make a positive difference in the lives of others—divine appointments presented for limited amounts of time. Only you can minister to those God has placed in your path in the unique way He has gifted you personally. The woman in today's story didn't ask for help; for various reasons, people in our lives won't always ask either.

How many windows of opportunity have we allowed to close because we didn't want to be interrupted from what we thought was more important? Sometimes we can focus on traditional "ministry" and fail to recognize a God-ordained opportunity to minister.

Life is constantly evolving. People won't always be in our lives, nor will they always be in their current situation. Circumstances change, conditions improve, people move on, and sadly, they pass away. ***They won't always need us like they do today.***

Is there a situation God is bringing to your mind? Perhaps something that has been gnawing at your conscience and bringing a nagging sense of moral obligation? What will you do? Ignore the problem, convince yourself it is none of your business or concern, or decide it is too messy to become involved? Or will you choose to follow Jesus' example and stop what you are doing to make a difference?

What if He had put the message He was teaching above the reason for the message? What if He had taught about healing yet allowed her to leave unhealed?

What or who will suffer if *you* don't mind God?

19

I CAN HEAL

"Bear ye one another's burdens, and so fulfill the law of Christ." Galatians 6:2

Feeling helpless as I stood by the bedside of both of my dying parents, watching loved ones suffer, and observing such pain in the lives of those around me, I have often thought about the miracles of healing Jesus and His disciples performed. I have longed to see such power demonstrated in these modern times and dreamed of walking through hospitals, stopping in every room, laying hands on the sick, and seeing miraculous answers to prayer. Though I have never witnessed or been privileged to be a part of such a widespread manifestation of miracles, the Lord opened my eyes to ways to bring a touch of healing to this hurting world by imitating four particular steps of Jesus.

First, Jesus always stopped what He was doing to give the person in front of Him His full, undivided attention.

I often become frustrated by the self-absorption so prevalent in our modern world. Social media has erected walls and insulated us from one another, as we take more interest in scrolling faces on our phones than face-to-face interaction. Empty, hurting people cross our paths, and we are too obsessed with checking online stats, "likes," and "dislikes" to even take notice. Long-term friendships suffer and wither from neglect as we pour ourselves into becoming online "friends" with people we have never even met.

Like Jesus, I can slow down enough to look into the windows of souls and stay aware of the people around me and their needs. I can stop running so fast through life and intentionally notice, no matter what important work I think I am doing. I can remove every distraction and listen from the heart. In these ways, I can heal.

Second, Jesus called others to Him.

His very persona sent the message of "Come unto Me." (Matthew 11:28). He was not offended or deterred by the severity of disease or sinful lifestyle of any person He ever encountered. In a human form, the very God of Heaven never looked down His nose on anyone, though He had every right. Though He is holiness and truth personified, His kind handling of sinners invited and attracted them to come to Him for help, deliverance, and forgiveness. I find it interesting that those who shied away from the Pharisees and religious leaders felt comfortable drawing near Jesus Christ.

I, too, can call others to a safe place. I cannot fix their problems, but I can point them to the One who can. By suspending judgment and looking at others through the eyes of Christ, I can draw them to the foot of His cross, where they will find the answer to their every need. In this way, I can heal.

Third, Jesus spoke healing words into hopeless situations.

No matter what challenge confronted Jesus, nothing was too hard for Him. He commanded the spirit of fear to leave the atmosphere by speaking life and light. "I will." "Why are ye fearful, O ye of little faith?" "Daughter, be of good comfort; thy faith hath made thee whole." "According to your faith be it unto you." "Peace, be still." "Be not afraid, only believe." "Be of good cheer: it is I; be not afraid." These are the life-giving responses Jesus often spoke to those who came to Him in desperate circumstances.

Proverbs 18:21 says, "Death and life *are* in the power of the tongue." We have all faced hard trials in life where fears have overwhelmed us, and it has felt like all is lost. How discouraging it is to have someone come along and confirm those fears by the thoughtless telling of gloom and doom past personal experiences or stories they have heard that did not end well! And how uplifting it is to hear life-giving words that fan the flame of flickering faith!

I can speak healing words by pointing those who are in despair to the Great Physician, the Healer, the Comforter, the One who has made such a positive difference in my life. I can speak the Word of God, reminding them there is hope, they can never be too far gone, and Jesus loves them so much He laid down His life and died for them. In this way, I can heal.

Fourth, Jesus touched them.

The human touch is dying in this modern age of push-button automation, and the lack thereof makes the world a cold and lonely place. 2 Corinthians 1:3-4 says, "Blessed *be* God, even the Father of our Lord Jesus Christ, the Father of mercies, and the God of all comfort, who comforteth us in all our tribulation, that we may be able to comfort them which are in any trouble, by the comfort wherewith we ourselves are comforted of God." The comforting touch of Jesus has ministered to my own hurting heart countless times throughout life. I can offer Him my hands and feet to reach the hopeless with that same gentle comfort.

In all these ways, I can heal, and so can you!

20

SOLITARY PLACES

"And in the morning, rising up a great while before day, He went out, and departed into a solitary place, and there prayed." Mark 1:35

I could never put into words how this verse moves and compels me to want to get alone with God in a solitary place and pray! Don't you wish you could have been there with Him? Wouldn't you love to know all He said in that early morning prayer? What was He asking of His Father? Or was He asking at all? Maybe He was praising and telling Him how much He missed being with Him in Heaven. We can only speculate because the Bible is silent on the content of most of Jesus' prayers. I love reading John 17, where it gives precise details of one of His openly spoken prayers—for Himself, for His disciples, and thank God, for us.

I've had some solitary places of my own through the years, alone with God. They have been some of the most precious times of communion with Him I have ever experienced. One of my favorite memories of such a place is a beach in Naples, FL. I was in my late teens and used to go there alone late in the evenings to sit on a boulder overlooking the Gulf of Mexico. I loved to get there in time to watch the sunset over the water—the scene was breathtaking, the presence of God so real.

Another favorite "alone with God" solitary place for me is in the mountains. Kevin and I used to ride a 4-wheeler to an isolated spot early in our marriage—he to look for deer, me to pray. He would drop me off at a particular place at the foot of a mountain where there were plenty of trees. It was remote, and I could pour my heart out to God, knowing He was the only one who would hear. After a while, Kevin would ride up on the 4-wheeler, and we would leave that hallowed spot. I think he took extra long sometimes, just because he hated to interrupt my time with the Lord.

These days, my solitary place is usually inside our home. Sometimes I am praising Him, sometimes there are tears, some are moments of intense worship, and then there are times that I stop and beg Him to **talk to me**. We all need two-way communication with God. So many times, we miss the most important part because we leave our knees or place of prayer too soon. *He* has things He wants to say to *us* if only we will get quiet enough to listen.

He speaks to the deep recesses of the soul—in that still small voice. That inner Monitor that says, "You're drifting too far from Me," and "Don't make that choice," and "This path will lead to Heaven, not that one." It is the voice of His precious Spirit. Jesus told His disciples in John 16:13, "Howbeit when He, the Spirit of truth, is come, He will guide you into all truth: for He shall not speak of Himself; but whatsoever He shall hear, *that* shall He speak: and He will shew you things to come." Notice it says, "whatsoever He shall hear that shall He *speak*."

The Spirit of God **speaks** to us, guiding us into all truth. The problem is, we live in a noisy world and stay engaged with activity and busyness. Constantly texting, scrolling, talking, listening, watching, and filling our minds, we don't make an effort to do what it takes to hear God's voice. How can we listen to Him when we bombard our ears, eyes, and minds with constant stimulation and commotion?

I wonder if the reason Jesus got up so early in the morning and found an utterly solitary place to pray is that He wanted to ***hear*** His Father's voice. His days were filled with constant activity from early morning until late night. Crowds of people were continually asking of Him, pulling at Him, wanting to hear Him talk, vying for His attention. Perhaps He knew He wouldn't be able to break away later in the day to commune with His Father, so He went out early to pray—while it was still and quiet before the world and all its noise was awake.

Getting alone with God requires us to turn off all noise, make ourselves unavailable to all other tasks, find a quiet and uninterrupted place, and get still and calm before Him. I often feel that compelling tug to a solitary place—to ask of Him, yes, but most of all to hear His voice.

21

YOU ASKED, DIDN'T YOU?

*"If ye then, being evil, know how to give good gifts unto your children, how much more shall your Father which is in Heaven give good things to them that **ask** him?" Matthew 7:11*

Have you ever been hesitant to ask God for something you wanted from Him? Or have you asked and then been completely surprised when He gave it to you?

One morning, I walked down the hall to where Zach was sitting in our den and asked him what he wanted for breakfast. I named off different meal choices, one being bacon, eggs, biscuits, and gravy. I know this is one of his favorite breakfast meals, so I wasn't surprised when his eyes lit up, and he said, "Yes, Mama. That sounds great!" Then I saw the light go out of his eyes, so I asked him what was wrong. He replied, "Well, no, never mind, I don't want to ask you that. It's just that I was craving something really bad." I said, "No, go ahead and tell me." He said, "Well, I am *really* craving your mayonnaise muffins. But, I don't want to make you do the extra work." I said, "Well, I have canned biscuits. Would that be okay for today?" He looked down, and even though I could see he was deeply disappointed, he said, "Okay, Mama. Canned biscuits will be fine."

I left the room without stating my final decision and went to the kitchen. I wasn't feeling the best, and it would have been so much easier to pop open the can of biscuits sitting in our refrigerator. But I didn't give it a second thought. Zach prefers my homemade muffins; he had asked for them, and by God's strength, I was bound and determined to make them for him.

I proceeded to cook breakfast, and a while later, he came down the hall into the kitchen. He walked over to the stove and peeked through the oven door window. The light was back in his eyes when he exclaimed, "Mama! You made mayonnaise muffins?" Joyfully I answered, "Of course I did! *You asked, didn't you*?"

Making mayonnaise muffins isn't such a difficult task. (I've included the recipe.) It doesn't take long, and seeing how happy it made Zach made the extra work all worthwhile.

We are often reluctant to ask our Heavenly Father for something we desire from Him because we feel we have asked too frequently for too much or that we don't deserve good things. We buy into satan's lies and feel intimidated to ask for the blessings God is so eager to bestow. James 4:2 says, "Ye have not, because ye ask not." And Luke 12:32 says, "Fear not, little flock; for it is your Father's good pleasure to give you the kingdom." How many blessings we miss out on because we do not do the simplest thing and ask!

When Kevin was going through a severe trial at work, the situation appeared to be too big for even God to fix, and we found ourselves so consumed with unbelief that it seemed pointless to ask. I will never forget the day things reached such an unbearable point that we dropped to our knees, side by side, and did what we had been so hesitant to do—we earnestly prayed and asked the Lord to fight for Kevin and bring relief. That prayer touched Heaven, God began to move, and it wasn't long until He completely resolved the situation. I wonder now if the trial may have ended much sooner if we had only asked.

It reminds me of the first verse of one of my favorite hymns, "What A Friend We Have In Jesus," written by Joseph A. Scrivens.

"What a friend we have in Jesus,

All our sins and griefs to bear!

What a privilege to carry,

Everything to God in prayer!

Oh, what peace we often forfeit,

Oh, what needless pain we bear,

All because we do not carry,

Everything to God in prayer!"

Ephesians 3:20 says, "Now unto Him that is able to do exceeding abundantly above all that we ask or think, according to the power that worketh in us."

God is able. That has never been the issue. ***The problem is that we do not ask.***

Recipe for Mayonnaise Muffins

2 cups self-rising flour

   1 cup milk

   ½ cup mayonnaise

Combine all ingredients. Stir until flour is moistened, but the batter is lumpy. Fill greased muffin tins ½ full. Bake at 450 degrees for 12-15 minutes. These are yummy, especially with butter, honey, and cinnamon sprinkled on them as soon as they come out of the oven. They also taste great with homemade gravy! Enjoy!

22

WHEN JESUS SEES US WEEP

"When Jesus, therefore, saw her weeping, and the Jews also weeping which came with her, He groaned in the spirit, and was troubled." John 11:33

Through the years, I have come to understand that compassion is a significant component of love. It brings about a deep empathy that runs through the inner heart—such that it moves and compels us to want to console and alleviate the pain of another, *no matter what the cost.*

Jesus' heart was full of this type of deep compassion, and it was one of the driving forces of His earthly ministry. Matthew 9:36 says, "But when He saw the multitudes, He was **moved with compassion** on them, because they fainted, and were scattered abroad, as sheep having no shepherd." Jesus did not merely *feel* inward compassion, but its intensity *moved* and compelled Him to action.

John 11:35 is one of the shortest verses in the Bible, containing only the two words "**Jesus wept.**" When I was a little girl, our Sunday School teacher used to ask us to memorize Bible verses so we could recite them in front of the congregation, and we all wanted to use John 11:35 because it was so short and easy to remember! Later, I realized those two brief words and the story surrounding them provide some of the most profound insights into the heart and personality of our Savior.

One of His dear friends, Lazarus, had been very ill, and even though Jesus knew he was sick, he had delayed going to see him. By the time He got there, Lazarus had been dead four days, and questions filled the minds of his family and loved ones. "Why didn't Jesus come sooner? Did He not care? Why has He been so silent and absent in our grief?" Their hearts were shattered, and Jesus' delay and lack of urgency to reach them were hard for them to understand.

When Jesus arrived and saw Lazarus' sister's anguish and his loved ones weeping and mourning, their grief affected Him so deeply that God in the flesh began to cry—right along with them. He did not weep because He was powerless to change their situation. He had all power. He could and still can do anything. He cried because it hurt so much to see *them* cry.

"When Jesus, therefore, saw her weeping, and the Jews also weeping which came with her, He groaned in the spirit, and was troubled." John 11:33

"When Jesus saw them weeping." Something about seeing their falling tears pained Him to the point that He could not stop the flow of His own. Tears wrenched from the human heart of our Lord and Master were mingled with the tears of the bereaved.

"For we have not an high priest which cannot be touched with the feeling of our infirmities; but was in all points tempted like as *we are, yet* without sin." Hebrews 4:15

He pities us. When we hurt, He is affected. **He feels what we feel.**

One day as we had family worship, Kevin prayed for Zach, his voice broke, and he could not speak for several seconds. His heart was so moved with compassion for our child that he could not hold back his tears. "Like as a father pitieth His children, so pitieth the Lord them that fear Him." Psalm 103:13

How blessed Zach is to have a father who prays for and pities him, and how blessed is the human race to have a Heavenly Father who not only sees every tear we cry, He even keeps a record of them!

Psalm 56:8 says, "Thou tellest my wanderings: put thou my tears into thy bottle: *are they* not in thy book?"

God sees every tear, even the silent ones that come unbidden when no one else sees. When the Lord called my dear Dad home to Heaven, I was 11 ½ weeks along in my pregnancy with Zach. I had never before and have never since experienced such a bittersweet time. Kevin and I barely had time to begin to anticipate Zach's birth, and then Dad was gone.

Like Lazarus' family, there were many questions in my mind. Why would God take Dad then, before he had a chance to see our baby? Zach is Dad's one and only biological grandchild. Why didn't Jesus heal Dad and allow him to be a part of Zach's life?

My heart was so broken, and due to previous health complications, my pregnancy was high risk. Friends, loved ones, and co-workers, out of concern and love for our unborn child and me, continually forbade me to cry. I had to do nearly all of my weeping in private. Otherwise, I would hear continual remarks like, "Don't cry, Cheryl. You'll hurt the baby." Or "Your baby will cry if you do —it will be affected. You can't do this." Kevin remembers the nights he heard me cry myself to sleep unhindered by the many comments of reproof I heard throughout the day.

I know Jesus noticed every tear that hit my pillow. I believe He gathered every one of them in His nail-scarred hands, put them in His bottle, and recorded each one of them in His book. And I believe His heart was moved with compassion as He witnessed my heartbreak.

Do you weep in silence, out of sight, alone in your inward pain? Do the ones closest to you fail to notice? Jesus sees your tears just as He saw Lazarus' loved ones weeping. With the same measure that He pitied them, so He pities you. He is seated at the right hand of the throne of His Father, constantly interceding—pleading for your relief. He is storing your tears in His bottle because they are valuable to Him. No one else may ever understand you or what you are going through, but He does—more than you will ever comprehend because **He remembers how it feels to cry.**

23

LEMONS & DIRT

"These things I have spoken unto you, that in Me ye might have peace. In the world ye shall have tribulation: but be of good cheer; I have overcome the world." John 16:33

The story of Joseph is one of my favorite stories in the Old Testament. If ever someone had a reason to become bitter, it was Joseph. After repeatedly dreaming at age 17 of being in authority over his parents and brothers, he ended up being betrayed by those same brothers and eventually sold as a slave to a foreign ruler. How he must have wondered about his dreams as he looked around at his unfamiliar surroundings, longed for home, and questioned the outcome of his life! But, despite all, he kept doing the right thing and made the best out of every bad situation. Near the end of his story, as he spoke to the very brothers who had betrayed him, he said, "But as for you, ye thought evil against me; *but* God meant it unto good." Genesis 50:20

The Bible doesn't say that life will be a bed of roses with no heartache, sickness, grief, or hurt. There are no promises of smooth sailing or a perfect picturesque existence. The important thing is how we react to the tribulations we must endure.

When writing an obituary for a dwarf actor in 1915, Elbert Hubbard said of him, "His was a sound mind in an unsound body. He proved the eternal paradox of things. He cashed in on his disabilities. He picked up the lemons that fate had sent him and started a lemonade stand."

And, we can learn much from the old story of the farmer and his mule.

"One day, a farmer's mule fell into a well. The animal cried piteously for hours as the farmer tried to figure out what to do. Finally, he decided the animal was old and the well needed to be covered up anyway. It just wasn't worth it to retrieve the mule. So he invited all his neighbors to come over and help him. They all grabbed a shovel and began to shovel dirt into the well. At first, the mule realized what was happening and cried horribly. Then, to everyone's amazement, he quieted down. A few shovel loads later, the farmer finally looked down the well and was astonished at what he saw. With every shovel of dirt that hit his back, the mule was doing something amazing. He would shake it off and take a step up, stomping the dirt under him. As the farmer's neighbors continued to shovel dirt on top of the animal, he would shake it off and take a step up. Pretty soon, everyone was amazed as the mule stepped up over the edge of the well and trotted off. He had used the very thing that was thrown at him to hurt him, to save his own life and get out of the well!" *Author Unknown*

We are all going to be dealt lemons and have dirt thrown on us from time to time.

"Be still, sad heart! and cease repining;

Behind the clouds is the sun still shining;

Thy fate is the common fate of all,

Into each life, some rain must fall." *Taken from "The Rainy Day" by Henry Wadsworth Longfellow*

There will always be cruel people who intend the things they say and do against us for evil, but God means it all for good. You may not see that today as you wonder how any good can come from the hard things you are walking through, but God has a plan, and in that plan, He must allow some rain to fall along with the sunshine for you to grow and develop into the person He wants you to be.

The question is, what will we do with the lemons and dirt? Will we allow them to make us sour and cynical against God and everyone around us, or will we follow the example of Joseph, the dwarf, and the mule and make lemonade amid bad situations? Will we allow the dirt people throw to bury us in self-pity, hatred, malice, and the desire for revenge? Or will we stomp it under our feet, rise above our circumstances, and use it to climb out of the hole?

24

EMPTY FEEDERS

"So when they had dined, Jesus saith to Simon Peter, 'Simon, son of Jonas, lovest thou Me more than these?' He saith unto him, 'Yea, Lord; thou knowest that I love thee.' He saith unto him, 'Feed My lambs.'" John 21:15

Kevin enjoys collecting birdfeeders. He had received several of them as gifts, but he hadn't been able to find the time to fill them or find a spot for them outside due to his work schedule. One day, while he and Zach were running errands, I surprised him by taking some of the feeders out of their packages and filling them for him. As I did, the Lord reminded me that by putting the food out for the birds, we were helping Him feed His creation.

I could picture the sweet, little creatures flying around, then landing on a branch of one of our trees and happily discovering the various goodies we had left behind. Envisioning that made me smile. Then it came to my mind how disappointed they would be to get used to finding nourishment there, only to come back later and find the feeders empty, and how important it is that we keep re-stocking the feeders regularly. I have heard that if a hummingbird comes to a feeder and finds it empty, it will not return.

In II Timothy 4:2, the Apostle Paul told Timothy to "Preach the word; be instant in season, out of season." In other words, at all times, in all situations, under all circumstances, Timothy needed to be ready to "feed" others. He needed to be prepared to minister to anyone he came across who was hungry for God and in need of spiritual help.

Some of Kevin's birdfeeders were eye-catching, and he strategically positioned them in places that he thought would be most visible to the birds he hoped to attract. No matter how colorful or appealing they were, they did the birds no good if they were empty.

The world is full of dry wells—places people go to fill the void in their hearts, only to find that sinful pleasures and false religion do not satisfy the hunger for God in the soul. They come away feeling emptier than ever, disillusioned and starving for something real. As Christians, they should be able to find that in us with our feeders continually full of the fruits of the Holy Spirit.

I Samuel 16:7 says, "For man looketh on the outward appearance, but the LORD looketh on the heart," and Proverbs 6:17 tells us that God hates a proud look. No matter how self-righteous we appear on the outside, He sees right through any form of pretense. If we profess to be something we are not, the people around us see right through it, too. The kind of fruit we bear in our everyday lives is the proof of our true selves.

When we sold our home and moved away, we left all of Kevin's birdfeeders behind. I wonder if the new owners of our former home still keep the feeders full. Or have they allowed them to hang empty, a disappointment to any bird looking for food? I wonder who may be looking to you and me, expecting to find our spiritual feeders full? What will they see when they take a closer look?

25

NEVER ALONE

"Abide with us: for it is toward evening, and the day is far spent." Luke 24:29

I sat with Mom in her living room, looking at old pictures and cards people had given her through the years. I am sure I had seen most or maybe all of them before, but it seemed important to her that I take each one of them, re-read them, and look at the pictures again. I got the feeling she just didn't want us to leave—that she was trying to find ways to keep me interested so Zach and I would stay a few minutes longer.

Mom lived alone, and she was very, very lonely. I remember through the years, one of her biggest fears was being alone in life. She left home and married at 18, and by the time her first husband died, she had four children. She was a widow, but she took comfort because she was a mother, and her children were still with her. A few years later, she married Dad, and at this time, one of my sisters was still living at home. One year later, I was born.

My sister married and left home when I was nine, and eleven years later, I left home and moved away. Then it was just Mom and Dad. When Dad passed away, for the first time, Mom's deep-grounded fears became a reality when she found herself utterly alone at age 72. It occurred to me one day that for 72 years, someone had always lived with Mom.

There is something about being in a house alone. The silence is deafening, and the feeling of isolation can be overwhelming. There is comfort in knowing someone familiar is living there, and when Mom no longer had that, it scared her.

During the nearly 12 years between the time Dad passed away and Mom died, Mom suffered a serious car accident that left her with three broken bones and in need of major surgery at the age of 77. She had a subsequent stroke immediately after surgery. She had an intestinal blockage which required major surgery at age 80, and another blockage and emergency surgery three years later at age 83. Each time, God's healing power was miraculous. He mercifully permitted her to recover, and even though she spent time in hospitals and rehab facilities, God enabled her to go home again to live alone at the end of each event.

Mom had to face the biggest fears of her life, and she was a real trooper. I used to hope she would find someone to share her life with after Dad died, but she lived out her remaining years alone. But was she alone? Jesus said He would never leave us nor forsake us—He is always there. Through every dark and lonely night, in every silent moment and each isolated scene, He stands close—watching, comforting, calming every fear, drying every tear.

One day, two men were walking the lonely 7 ½ mile trek between Jerusalem and Emmaus. Their hearts were sad and grieving because Jesus, the One they followed and whom they had hoped was the Messiah, had been brutally killed by cruel men. They were disillusioned, disappointed, and not sure what to do next. They felt very much alone and completely forsaken.

As they walked along, Jesus Himself drew near and began to walk along with them. They didn't recognize Him. Their hearts were so broken, it probably never even occurred to them who He was. In their minds, Jesus, standing there in the flesh, walking alongside them, was not even a remote possibility. He asked them why they were sad. They found it unbelievable that anyone could be in that area and not know why they were sad!

He listened as they vented their frustrations, and then He began to speak—words of life and hope and encouragement. He spoke of Moses and all the prophets and expounded all that had been written and foretold about Him. They listened with rapt attention until they reached their destination in the village of Emmaus. As they slowed their pace to go into the house, Jesus kept walking. Something in the two men could not let Him go—they longed for His presence and the comfort of simply having Him with them. "Abide with us," they invited, as He walked away. All He needed was an invitation.

He went into the house with them, and as they sat down to eat dinner, their eyes were opened when He blessed the meal. Finally, they recognized who He was! After He vanished out of their presence, they asked one another, "Did not our hearts burn within us, while He talked with us by the way, and while He opened to us the Scriptures?" Luke 24:32

They were not alone! They had seen the Lord, and He had walked and talked with them! He had risen from the dead, and there was hope! They were so refreshed in spirit that they left and walked the 7 ½ miles back to Jerusalem the same night!

It comforts me to know that Jesus will always show up during the loneliest, most isolated moments of our lives. He will draw near as we walk in quiet sadness. He will appear on the scene and offer hope. He will remind us of His Word and all the promises and comfort we can find in it. His presence is real, and we will find that we never want Him to leave. Our hearts will burn within us with renewed courage to walk another mile as we hear the soothing comfort of His voice.

Mom may have been the only one living in her little apartment, but Mom was not alone—not for even a moment. Nights were the worst times for her, but she used to tell me how God would bring comforting songs and Scriptures to her mind in the night when she was awake and couldn't sleep. I could just picture Jesus standing there whispering them to her in the darkness, encouraging her, reminding her He was there and always would be.

Do you feel lonely and abandoned? Are you faced with the cold, harsh reality of being alone when you go to bed each night? Do you long for the days when there was someone with you? There *is* Someone there. Your sadness may be so intense that you, as the men on the way to Emmaus, do not recognize Him, but He is there abiding with you—and He will never leave.

26

THE NEXT PAGE

"And they commanded the people, saying, 'When ye see the ark of the covenant of the LORD your God, and the priests the Levites bearing it, then ye shall remove from your place, and go after it. Yet there shall be a space between you and it, about two thousand cubits by measure: come not near unto it, that ye may know the way by which ye must go: **for ye have not passed this way heretofore."**
Joshua 3:3,4

I sat at the kitchen table, tears threatening to spill any moment. I felt so sorry for Zach. He was seated in the chair next to me, and it was painful to watch him become more and more frustrated over his school work. He was working on math problems that he was familiar with and knew how to solve, and the page was half-finished, so I wondered why he was becoming more and more agitated. Finally, I asked him what was wrong.

"Mama!" he exclaimed as he flipped his workbook over to the next page. When I saw it, I knew instantly why his little heart was so troubled. On the next page was brand-new information—problems he'd never seen or had to solve before, and he was filled with anxiety. He was heading into unknown, uncharted territory, and even though he hadn't reached that point yet and was still working on a page that was easy for him, he had looked ahead and seen what was coming, and the dread of it was overwhelming him.

I said, "Zach, don't worry about that page right now. Just work on the page you are on. Finish that first, and then we'll do the next page together." He reluctantly went back to doing what was familiar and comfortable, and when he finished that page, we tackled the next one. He caught on quickly, and it turned out his dread was entirely unnecessary. He even said it was fun!

It hurts me to see him get so upset and worried over what's coming next. I could look at the page he was so troubled about, and to me, it was no mystery. I already knew how to solve the problems, so they didn't threaten me the way they intimidated Zach. I tried to tell him that it wasn't that bad and that I would be there with him and help him through it. But, to him, it was monumental and frightening, and it disturbed him terribly.

I've always been prone to worry over the future and sometimes wake up in full-blown panic attacks—not necessarily over things happening, but because of what I fear **might** happen. Even though things are calm around me, the fear and dread of what might happen on the "next page" causes me not to enjoy the peaceful setting I am in today.

In Joshua 3:3,4, God told Joshua to tell the children of Israel that they were to faithfully follow the Ark of the Covenant and the priests carrying it. When the Ark moved, the people were to move.

When it stopped, they were to stop. They were always to stay 2,000 cubits (about ½ mile) **behind the Ark**. Verse 4 ends by saying, "for ye have not passed this way heretofore." God's presence, represented by the Ark of the Covenant, was going out in front of them, and the Israelites didn't have to figure things out on their own. All they had to do was stay **behind the Ark** and follow God's lead.

In Matthew 6:34, Jesus said, "Take therefore no thought for the morrow: for the morrow shall take thought for the things of itself. Sufficient unto the day *is* the evil thereof." The "page" in front of us has enough problems of its own, and we are not to worry about what is on the next. We have not passed this way before. We don't know what the future holds, but God is in front of us. He sees what is on the next page, all the way to the end of our earthly days. The future doesn't intimidate or surprise Him at all. Since He knows all the answers, you and I have nothing to fear.

27

FORGOTTEN BENEFITS

"Bless the LORD, O my soul, and forget not all His benefits." Psalm 103:2

When Kevin worked the 3rd shift and had to travel almost 60 miles round trip to and from work, I worried incessantly over him driving late at night on the deserted country roads between his workplace and home. Besides obvious reasons for concern, the deer population was abundant in our area. As I prayed daily for God's protection, I consistently asked Him to "remove deer from Kevin's path."

One night, while on his way home, Kevin called, and when I answered the phone, I knew right away something was wrong. He sounded shaken as he said, "I hit a deer." After I asked him if he was okay, he responded, "Yeah, I'm fine," and then went on to tell me what happened.

He was driving along at about 60 mph and decided to change over to the passing lane to pass the car in front of him. When he got just about even with the car he was passing, an adult-size deer ran out in front of the car beside him! By the time the deer reached the lane Kevin was in, it was injured and lying on the ground. The only way it made contact with our car, is when Kevin had no choice but to run over it. He and the lady driving the other vehicle pulled over, and right away, Kevin could see that her car was badly damaged. When he looked at our car, he saw absolutely no harm done—not even a dent! As I listened to him telling me what happened, my mind immediately went back to the many times I had prayed that prayer. How many other deer has God removed from Kevin's path? We knew about this one, and we fervently gave God thanks, but what about all the other times God brought him home safe without hitting a deer?

I am careful to thank God often for the blessings I remember, but what about all the benefits I am not even aware of or forget?

What about all the times God has answered a prayer prayed in a moment of panic, and I completely forgot to go back and give Him thanks? What about the unexpected card I got in the mail from a long-lost friend? What about the dove that landed unexpectedly on the roof of my car during a troubled time? What about the deer that was hit by another vehicle instead of ours?

In Luke 17:11-19, we find a story about ten lepers who, seeing Jesus from afar, lifted their voices and said, "Jesus, Master, have mercy on us." Leprosy was a debilitating disease, and those who suffered from it were forced to live tormented lives, isolated from family and friends. In response to their cries for mercy, Jesus told them to go and show themselves to the priest according to Old Testament procedures for someone healed of leprosy. As they walked away in obedience to Jesus' command, all ten lepers were instantly healed! It was a miracle of monumental proportions and truly amazing to behold. They got their lives back! No longer outcasts, they could return home to their wives and families and resume a normal life. One would think these ten former lepers would be the most grateful men on earth, but astonishingly only one of the men "turned back, and with a loud voice glorified God, and fell on his face at Jesus' feet, giving Him thanks." Jesus asked the man, "Were there not ten cleansed? But *where are the nine*?"

I look at these nine men with a feeling close to contempt. How could they? After what Jesus did for them, how could they walk away in good conscience and never turn around and say, "thank you?" It seems inconceivable until I pause to consider my own ingratitude and the many benefits I have forgotten. How many times have I failed to turn back and give Him thanks?

Now and then, it is a good idea to bow our heads and thank God for forgotten benefits, such as:

- So many answers to prayer
- Countless times of protection when we didn't realize we were in jeopardy
- Times He rearranged our day, so we didn't have an accident
- Every detour He orchestrated to keep us from being exposed to sickness
- Every temptation He helped us avoid
- Every time He saved our lives from shipwreck, and the list goes on perpetually.

So many benefits. Such a merciful God. Very forgetful me.

Shamefully, I feel like I have a lot of remembering and thanking to do, and I can't think of a better time to start than right now.

28

DIGGING OLD WELLS

"As the hart panteth after the water brooks, so panteth my soul after thee, O God." Psalm 42:1

I was feeling drained and lean in my soul. I tried to pray, but it seemed the heavens were brass. I picked up my Bible, seeking inspiration, only to find I couldn't focus or glean anything beneficial. Time after time, the soul within me felt exceedingly thirsty for God, but I just couldn't seem to feel His presence at all. I desperately missed the encouragement I usually received during my time with Him, and I remember asking, "Lord, are You angry with me?" There just seemed to be such a distance between us, an impenetrable wall that had somehow been erected, and I could not remember doing anything that would cause such a breach.

One day, I picked up my Bible and read the story found in Genesis 26:1-19. After Isaac moved near Abimelech in the land of the Philistines, the Lord abundantly blessed him and increased his goods to the point that the Philistines who lived around him became jealous and wanted him to leave. So, he moved a distance away and pitched his tent in the valley of Gerar.

In Gerar, he found some wells dug by his father, Abraham's servants, years before. At one time, they had provided cool, refreshing water for his father, his family, and their livestock. But, after Abraham's death, the Philistines had come along and filled the wells with dirt, stifling the flow and purpose of the refreshing water beneath. When Isaac discovered the wells and what had happened to them, verses 18 & 19 say that he "digged again the wells of water, which they had digged in the days of Abraham his father, and he called them their names after the names by which his father had called them, and Isaac's servants digged in the valley and found there a well of springing water."

The term "springing water" literally means "living water!"

Imagine the joy of seeing the wells that were once hindered and clogged by dirt once again springing up with thirst-quenching, life-sustaining water! It must have filled Isaac's heart with unspeakable joy to find these wells and then be able to cleanse them of obstructions and make them usable again.

As I read this story, God began to open my eyes to the reason for my spiritual dryness. He showed me that I had allowed the enemy to come along somewhere along the line and fill up my spiritual wells—with hurt, resentment, indifference, offense, discouragement, neglect, and a host of other things. At the time, I hadn't realized what was happening, but, slowly, little by little, the "dirt" kept coming, and eventually, the life-sustaining flow of living water had been stopped up and stifled in my soul. The joy was gone, and I was thirsty.

I prayed Psalm 42:1. I cried out to God and told Him how thirsty I was for Him—weary from enemy pursuit, my soul was parched and panting for Him like a thirsty deer who came upon a refreshing water brook after being chased by a relentless hunter. And, I began to dig.

Shovelful by shovelful, I dug out the things the enemy had used to stop up my spiritual well. I let go of the hurt and chose to forgive. I decided resentment just wasn't worth the effort it took to keep around, so I dug it out and tossed it on the growing pile beside my well. I cringed as I saw how indifferent I had become, so I tore down the wall of defense I had built and watched it shatter on top of the "dirt" pile. I dug out offenses and handed them to Jesus, as He gently reminded me of the unjust way He was treated. As the last bit of dirt was removed and flung to the top of the pile, John 4:14 water began flowing unhindered once again in my soul. "But whosoever drinketh of the water that I shall give him shall never thirst, but the water that I shall give him shall be in him a well of water springing up into everlasting life." Joy over feeling His presence again flooded my soul, and Isaiah 12:3 came alive to me. "Therefore with joy shall ye draw water out of the wells of salvation."

Well-digging is hard work. It requires dedication and perseverance, and the will to keep going until every bit of "dirt" is removed, but the end result will bring showers of blessing. Jesus is still the eternal, artesian source of living water, and He has a never-ending supply. All we need to do is rediscover and re-dig our old wells and get rid of the dirt.

29

GUARD RAILS

"Remove not the ancient landmark, which thy fathers have set." Proverbs 22:28

The rain poured down as we traveled north after visiting Dad's family in Tennessee. I was five years old. My 13-year old sister, Debbie, and I were riding in our car's back seat, Dad was driving, and Mom was in the front passenger seat. Those were the days before wearing seat belts was mandatory, and I don't remember if our old car even had them!

As we drove along, the rain intensified, and the temperature began to drop, making for very treacherous driving conditions. All of a sudden, still going full-interstate-legal-speed, our car started sliding. Before we knew what was happening, Dad began to lose control. We were driving through a very mountainous stretch of highway, and there was a huge drop-off at the side of the road.

As we careened across our lane, we slid into the shoulder of the road, and our car hit the guard rail. I still have memories of feeling the tremendous jolt as our car and the guard rail collided. The impact of making contact at such high speed started our car spinning around, and when we finally stopped spinning, we found ourselves headed in the wrong direction, facing oncoming traffic!

I will never forget the feeling of being tossed from one side of the back seat to the other and the fear and panic I felt as I looked ahead and saw fast-moving cars heading straight toward us. Dad was level-headed and was able, by God's grace and mercy, to quickly get our car turned back around, going in the right direction to avoid crashing into the oncoming traffic.

I remember how we pulled off the interstate at the next exit and stopped at a service station. The man told us he was surprised our car had kept going because of something shaken loose under the hood. I can't remember the details, but I distinctly remember all of us giving thanks to God for the great mercy He had just extended. We were bruised and shaken, but thankfully, none of us were seriously hurt.

I have often thought about and relived that accident and wondered about many "what-ifs." What if whatever had shaken loose had caused our car to stall in the middle of the road? What if that had happened when we were facing oncoming traffic? What if Dad hadn't been so quick to know what to do? What if he had frozen in panic? What if those cars had been closer to us when we spun around to face them?

But, my biggest "what if" question has always been, **"What if that guard rail hadn't been there?"** What if we had wrecked at a spot on that highway where there was no guard rail? If we had slid off the road at one of those points, we probably wouldn't have been found for who knows how long, and more than likely, none of us would be here today to tell about it.

Our violent collision into the guard rail knocked us off-course, and the shock of it was overwhelming. But, the crash caused two positive things to happen—it saved us from falling to certain death, and it instantly got our attention. There was no ignoring or denying the impact of that crash.

Thinking back on that guard rail reminds me of life. In His Word, God has set landmarks and placed boundaries that we should never cross. Surrounding these parameters are guard rails that God uses as wake-up calls to keep us from careening over the ledge. When we begin to drift and waver and vary from the straight and narrow path, He will allow us to collide with these protective guard rails for two reasons: to save us from falling to certain eternal death and to get our attention. Because of His great love for us, He will permit certain things to happen in our lives to wake us up and give us an opportunity to get back on course.

We can sometimes view our "wake-up-call-collisions" with God's guard rails as restrictive inconveniences and interruptions to our carefully laid plans. We wonder why God won't let us have our way without accompanying guilt feelings and jolts to our conscience. We sometimes long for Him to let us run free without parameters. We wonder why we can't do anything and everything we want without feeling reproved for sin. The truth is, God loves us too much to fail to warn us of the horrors that await those who spend eternity without Him.

When we made contact with the guard rail, Dad could have complained about the damage the crash did to our car. He could have grumbled about the cost of the repair or the inconvenience of getting it fixed. I don't remember him doing any of that. *He was too busy thanking God that the guard rail was there* and that it kept us from something far worse.

Guard rails should not be moved. They are there for our protection. And, we can't afford to remove God's ancient landmarks or to ignore our collisions with the "guard rails" that surround them. Though a crash into a spiritual guard rail is not pleasant, it is God's mercy in disguise.

My family experienced the benefit of a guard rail first-hand that rainy day. Its stability and immovability helped save all of our physical lives. As I look back over my life and recall collisions with spiritual guard rails, I realize God's mercy placed them there for my protection—*not to fence me in but to keep danger out.*

30

OUR FOOTPRINTS

"Train up a child in the way he should go: and when he is old, he will not depart from it." Proverbs 22:6

Someone is stepping into the footprints we are leaving behind.

When Zachary was little, I heard him say, "Daddy, you're my hero. I want to be just like you!" It touched my heart because there is no human on earth that I would rather our son pattern himself after than his father. Kevin is the kindest, gentlest man I know. I am so thankful that even now, Zach wants to be just like him.

As I listened to Zach's words that day, I realized what an immense responsibility it to is to have someone want to be "just like us." No matter who we are, we are influencing someone. Our actions are having an impact on at least one other person. We are teaching by example, whether good or bad, especially as parents. Our children look up to us, and we are their role models—it automatically comes with the territory.

Nothing in my life has ever helped me spiritually as much as having a child. Not long after Zach was born, I remember looking down into his innocent, trusting face as I rocked him to sleep and realizing that his eternal soul was entrusted to Kevin's and my safekeeping, and we would be held accountable for his spiritual training. Though other parenting responsibilities felt somewhat daunting, the charge of "training up a child in the way he should go" was overwhelming. It occurred to me that the way he would be most strongly taught and greatly influenced is through the way Kevin and I naturally live out our lives day by day. I will forever be grateful to God for entrusting the gift of parenthood to us and for the element of spiritual accountability it continually brings to my daily life. Being Zachary's mother compels me to walk more carefully before the Lord and to strive to be a better person—a better Christian.

The Apostle Paul said in I Corinthians 11:1, "Be ye followers of me, even as I also am of Christ." As adults, we can distinguish between whether or not someone we admire is following Christ and whether it is safe for us to follow their example. Our children automatically look up to and follow us without realizing they need to make that distinction.

Dad used to tell me that a child is like a twig planted in the ground. It is bendable, and whatever direction it is bent as a twig will determine the direction it grows as a tree. One day when our children are grown, if we live long enough, we will see what they become, and no doubt, we will recognize fragments and effects of ourselves mirrored in them. Will we be proud or ashamed?

While they are still in the formative "twig" stage of life, we can prevent regrets by correcting wrong courses in our own lives to present a godly pattern for them to safely model. We cannot control their adult life choices or the outcome, but we can certainly do our best to mind God and point them in the right direction.

Who are you influencing? Whether or not you are a parent, who motivates you to live a more careful life? Who wants to be "just like you?" Is there a child, grandchild, sibling, niece, nephew, Sunday School student, co-worker, friend, or someone else who looks up to you and follows in your footsteps? Take a mental assessment of the people in your life and evaluate your performance. Acknowledging there is someone with a soul bound for eternity counting on us to do the right thing is sobering but of great importance. Does our daily example teach them to be more like Jesus?

31

SISTER ROSE

"They helped every one his neighbor; and every one said to his brother, 'Be of good courage.'" Isaiah 41:7

I still remember when I met her. I was an 11-year-old sixth-grader, self-conscious, timid, and insecure from changing schools far too many times. Regardless of how often it happened, it never failed to make me extremely anxious to face my first day in a new school, and that day was no exception.

I walked into the basement of the church nervous and filled with dread. When I got to the classroom, she was one of the first people I met and introduced herself as Sister Rose. I didn't know it then, but she would become a role model, leave a permanent impression on my life, and end up being a source of encouragement to me through the years.

She seemed to understand me, and I think she took extra time to make me feel at ease and welcome in my new surroundings. As I became better acquainted with her, I learned that she had never married, but she had, up to that point, devoted her life to missionary work and teaching in Christian Schools. Sister Rose was entirely sold-out for God, and His Spirit permeated everything about her. Just being around her made me want to live a better life.

We never stayed in one place for too long, and after I left the school where she taught, we completely lost touch. Imagine my surprise when, eleven years later, I was attending a camp meeting and spotted someone who looked familiar! Could it be? After all, I knew her in Ohio, and we were in Florida. I drew closer to her, and yes, it was my beloved childhood teacher, Sister Rose! Remarkably, she remembered me, and what a blessing it was to talk to her and find that she was still as in love with Jesus as ever! Her steadfastness and consistent Christian life motivated me to seek that same stability in my own Christian experience. She told me she had gotten married, but sadly, her husband had passed away.

From time to time, we talked on the phone after that, and during our talks, I learned that she had happily remarried a wonderful Christian man. When I later heard that he had also passed away, I called her with intentions of being an encouragement and offering my condolences.

Her voice sounded as cheerful as ever when she answered the phone, and instead of me encouraging her, she encouraged me! I found her trust in God to be as unshaken as ever. No questioning "why me?" or "I don't understand why God allowed this to happen—again." What I heard was sweet resignation to the divine will of God, and instead of her wanting to talk of her burdens, she wanted to hear about mine. When I finished pouring out my heart, she said, "Cheryl, you're doing the right thing. You're doing a good job." Oh, how I needed those words of affirmation!

Dear, faithful Sister Rose! Right amid her own grief, she found words of comfort for someone else. Before we hung up, I told her how much her consistent life for God has meant to me, and she told me how much she appreciated me saying that. I have a hunch that she needed encouragement after all.

Ira Sankey told this story.

"*During the recent war in the Transvaal,*" *said a gentleman at my meeting in Exeter Hall, London, in 1900, "when the soldiers going to the front were passing another body of soldiers whom they recognized, their greetings used to be, 'Four-nine-four, boys; four-nine-four;' and the salute would invariably be answered with 'Six further on, boys; six further on.' The significance of this was that, in 'Sacred Songs and Solos,' a number of copies of the small edition of which had been sent to the front, number 494 was 'God Be With You Until We Meet Again' and six further on than 494, or number 500, was 'Blessed Assurance, Jesus is mine.'"*

To maintain their morale, the soldiers would call out these encouraging words as they passed one another!

We all need encouragement, and some people are natural-born encouragers. Some of those special people have often held my feet to the fire and encouraged me to go on. When I think of them, my mind always turns to my sweet childhood teacher and lifelong friend, Sister Rose.

32

RESTING WITH THE SHEPHERD

"And He said unto them, 'Come ye yourselves apart into a desert place and rest awhile.'" Mark 6:31

After many busy years in full-time Christian service and running full-speed ahead, Jesus gently called my family and me "apart into a desert place" to rest a while. Though I had resisted at first, I finally stopped struggling against that "call apart" and yielded to His invitation to fall back into His arms and allow Him to hold me fast.

As our Shepherd, Jesus knows when enough is enough. He knows when we are completely spent and in need of rest. When we don't have enough foresight to see that we are on the brink of complete burnout, He does. So, He calls us aside, away from the noise and demands, and He bids us be still.

When Jesus called His disciples to the desert, He did so from a place of deep concern. They had just received the dreadful, traumatizing news that John the Baptist had been beheaded, then gone to the prison to retrieve his body and given him a proper burial. On top of such deep grief, they had been stretched and sought after to the point of exhaustion. Verse 31 goes on to say, "... for there were many coming and going, and they had no leisure so much as to eat."

Nothing escaped Jesus' watchful, careful eye. He loved these men. They were His faithful, loyal followers, the very ones who would carry on His work after He was gone, and He cared deeply about their needs. He recognized that their nerves and physical bodies were in dire need of nourishment, healing, and restoration. They weren't complaining, but Jesus knew it was time to pull them aside.

God knows when we need to rest, and He will do what is best to cause that to happen. Sometimes we see these "calls aside" as unnecessary, annoying interruptions of our busy lives and schedules. We may long to be back on the active battlefield, when all along, He sees that one more minute in the fray would be one minute too many. None of us are so strong that we can run wide-open with no reprieve and no time to reload.

If God pulls us to the sidelines, it is because He wants to draw us close to Himself.

Isaiah 32:18 says, "And My people shall dwell in a peaceable habitation, and in sure dwellings, and in quiet resting places." Tucked away from the rush and bustle and stress of this busy world, God has quiet resting places for His people. Areas where He deals with us one-on-one, with no noise or interruption. Sites where He feeds us and applies His healing balm to our wounds and weary hearts. Places where He mends the brokenness in us and restores the tattered places in our soul.

In John 10:27, Jesus said, "My sheep hear My voice, and I know them, and they follow Me." If the Shepherd calls you to come apart into a desert place and rest awhile, don't resist. Maybe He is allowing a physical affliction or handicap to slow you down, or He has permitted a hurt to strike deep within your heart to pull you to His arms. Perhaps your carefully laid plans have been shattered and rearranged, or maybe He just gave you a gentle nudge to "come aside" with Him to a desert place.

At first glance, the desert seems like nothing more than a dry, barren wasteland. No beautiful flowers to gaze upon, no refreshing wells to drink from, nothing living. But, oh, the treasures that await when the Shepherd takes us there! Time slows down to a crawl—with nothing else to do but listen to the soothing sound of His voice teaching, encouraging, calming, and reassuring us that there are better days ahead.

33

CHRISTMAS FROM THE DUMPSTER

"Every good gift and every perfect gift is from above and cometh down from the Father of lights." James 1:17

I don't remember the exact year, but I was somewhere around four or five years old. Christmas was coming, and due to our lean finances, no one in our household had any idea how we would buy gifts. We had pretty much decided there wouldn't be much of a Christmas—but then, in a very unexpected way, everything changed.

Dad used to describe himself as a "jack-of-all-trades, yet master of none." When something broke in our household, we usually couldn't afford to call a professional, so Dad would tackle the job himself. He was a star pupil in the school of hard knocks, and the by-product of his many years working in maintenance and do-it-yourself necessity was that he had developed skills in plumbing, electrical, car mechanics, and all types of home maintenance. He was the best improviser I have ever known. He could take almost anything broken and rig up some way to fix it. If he didn't have the right parts, he would create them out of the most unlikely objects. Dad could do a lot of things, but one of his most enjoyable "skills" involved trash-picking.

Yes, my dear Dad loved to pick through the trash. He loved to see if there was anything salvageable that he could reinvent, re-use, or recycle into something useful. He could very easily have been the man who coined the phrase, "One man's trash is another man's treasure."

Dad was a very humble man, so jobs that other people find demeaning didn't affect him or make him feel degraded in the least. He wasn't one for caring what other people thought of or said about him, and he didn't have an ounce of foolish pride. Just accepting things as they were, Dad made the best of the hand he had been dealt. One of the many jobs he held through the years was riding on the back of a garbage truck for the sanitation department.

Despite the stench and filth, it was one of his favorite jobs because of the "goodies" he would come across. One day he came home with a beautiful crocheted afghan that someone had carelessly tossed on the top of their trash. Mom washed it thoroughly, and my family used it for years. I still remember its vibrant color scheme and how pretty it looked on the back of our couch.

Dad had a friend named Jimmy who would sometimes join him in his trash-picking endeavors. Dad was husky and strong, and Jimmy was considerably thinner and more limber. During Dad and Jimmy's trash-picking escapades, Dad would stand outside a garbage dumpster, and Jimmy would climb onto Dad's shoulders and dive in.

Jimmy's family was struggling, too, and he and his wife had two little boys who were close to my age. Desperate times call for desperate measures, so right before the Christmas mentioned above, Dad and Jimmy decided to go trash-picking. In their search, they came across a toy store and stumbled upon a dumpster treasure trove in the back of the store! Now that I am grown and know how much it means to Kevin and me to see the thrill in Zach's eyes at Christmas, I can only imagine how Dad and Jimmy felt when they discovered what was in that dumpster. It must have felt like the ultimate trash-picking score!

Once again, Jimmy climbed onto Dad's shoulders while Dad stood outside the dumpster. Toy after toy came to the surface as Jimmy searched through the rubbish. All of them had some slight defect, just enough to make them "unsellable," but they were brand-new in their original boxes! They brought the toys home, and what a Christmas we had! I will never forget the thrill in my heart when my Daddy handed me a beautiful Snow White doll that talked when you pulled her string. Even though she had a minor imperfection and stuttered a bit, it never made any difference to me. For years, I loved and cherished her, and she and I spent many happy hours together.

Christmas was extra special that year, and I remember it as being one of the happiest of my childhood. It didn't matter to any of us where our toys came from—to us, they were good and perfect gifts, and we were deeply grateful.

After all, every good and perfect gift comes straight from Him, no matter where we find it.

34

THE POWER OF SONG

"I will sing a new song unto thee, O God: upon a psaltery and an instrument of ten strings will I sing praises unto thee." Psalm 144:9

When I was growing up, music was always an integral part of our lives. Since Mom and Dad both loved bluegrass, I developed a deep love for it, too. I grew up listening to Reno & Smiley, The Stanley Brothers, The Louvin Brothers, Flatt & Scruggs, Bill Monroe, The Osborne Brothers, Mac Wiseman, The Seldom Scene, The Country Gentlemen, Jim and Jesse, and many others. Every Saturday night, we looked forward to the bluegrass show on WYSO radio station in Yellow Springs, Ohio. We also loved listening to a DJ named Moon Mullins on WPFB in Middletown, Ohio. He had a group named "The Boys from Indiana," and I will never forget a sad American Civil War song they sang called "Atlanta is Burning." It was on the

Moon Mullins show that I first heard the voice of my favorite singer of all time, Ricky Skaggs.

Dad played the five-string banjo and guitar, and several of my uncles, cousins, and other relatives played various musical instruments. Many of us sang, and all of our family gatherings centered around making the music we all knew and loved.

I still remember the first time I sang harmony. Back then, we didn't wear seat belts, so when our family rode together in the car, my habit was to prop my little elbows on the back of the front seat and poke my head between Mom and Dad. Time spent in our car was often accompanied by music, and on that particular day, Mom and Dad were singing "Amazing Grace." I still remember how they looked at each other when out of the blue, I began to chime in, singing pitch-perfect tenor! I was three years old.

Mom, Dad, and so many of the ones we used to sing and play music with have passed on to their Heavenly home, and one of the ways I keep their memory alive is through the music I still listen to and sing today. Those dear, old songs take me away—back to a place in a childhood filled with so many sweet memories, smiling faces, and happy times. I never hear the sound of a banjo that I don't think of Dad and miss him and Mom.

When Kevin and I started dating, I was so thrilled to find that he, too, has a deep love of bluegrass and is familiar with all the old groups and songs that were an integral part of my upbringing. We sing and do a lot of listening together and always enjoy gathering with others who do the same.

Music has a way of stirring our emotions and taking us back to moments in the past. It is also very therapeutic and a wonderful way to draw our hearts into a place of worship. The Apostle Paul said in Ephesians 5:19, "Speaking to yourselves in psalms and hymns and spiritual songs, singing and making melody in your heart to the Lord." Psalm 33:2,3 says, "Praise the LORD with harp: sing unto Him with the psaltery *and* an instrument of ten strings. Sing unto Him a new song; play skilfully with a loud noise."

In the Bible, singing, playing instruments, and praising God invoked His glory to descend upon the congregation in a powerful way. 2 Chronicles 5:13, 14 says, "It came even to pass, as the trumpeters and singers *were* as one, to make one sound to be heard in praising and thanking the LORD; and when they lifted up *their* voice with the trumpets and cymbals and instruments of music, and praised the LORD, *saying*, 'For He is good; for His mercy *endureth* for ever: that *then* the house was filled with a cloud, *even* the house of the LORD; So that the priests could not stand to minister by reason of the cloud: for the glory of the LORD had filled the house of God."

In 2 Chronicles 20:21,22, we read of the time King Jehoshaphat strategically placed singers on the frontlines of a battle. "And when he had consulted with the people, he appointed singers unto the LORD, and that should praise the beauty of holiness, as they went out before the army, and to say, 'Praise the LORD; for His mercy endureth forever.' And when they began to sing and to praise, the LORD set ambushments against the children of Ammon, Moab, and mount Seir, which were come against Judah; and they were smitten. " The only weapons they used were songs of praise, and God fought their battle for them by setting ambushments and destroying their enemies!

Isaiah 61:3 says Jesus came to give us "**the garment of praise for the spirit of heaviness.**" The very antidote to the heaviness that often envelops and weighs us down is to put on the garment of praise. If we approach our battles with worship and magnify His name through song, He will fight our battles for us just as He fought for King Jehoshaphat. "Jesus Christ *is* the same yesterday, today, and forever." Hebrews 13:8 (NKJV) "For there is no respect of persons with God." Romans 2:11

There are many songs in my heart, each one with special memories attached. Old songs from childhood sung with family and loved ones, songs God has inspired me to write, and beautiful hymns I have learned and held dear through the years. I cherish them all and miss the ones who used to sing with me. One day we will reunite around God's throne and worship Him forever. Until then, I will continue praising Him and keeping those old memories alive through the songs we used to sing.

35

PRINCESS

"For He shall give his angels charge over thee, to keep thee in all thy ways." Psalm 91:11

For a time, we lived in a farmhouse situated at the end of a long dirt lane. While living there, our dog, Princess, came into our lives. She was a beautiful, purebred German Shepherd, and she became an "angel" of sorts to my family and me. I was still too young to go to school, so she and I spent many happy hours running and exploring the many outbuildings on the farm.

My older sister, Debbie, walked down the lane each morning to catch the bus to ride to school, and I would often walk along with her. Princess was always at our side, and each time, she would do the most remarkable thing. When we reached the road at the end of the lane, Princess would walk ahead of Debbie and me and stand sideways, creating a protective barrier between us and the road. When the bus arrived, she would move aside, but only to allow Debbie enough room to pass and get on the bus. As the bus drove away, Princess and I would walk back down the lane together toward home. Her protective nature was truly extraordinary, and Mom always felt safe for me to be outside as long as she was with me.

As a young child, I loved to "play" church. One day, I gathered all my dolls and stuffed animals and decided we would all go outside to one of my favorite outbuildings and have a church service! I can still see Mom standing at the kitchen counter making supper as I passed her on my way out the back door. I walked outside, down the back steps to the outbuilding located not too far from the back of the house, and I went inside.

I placed my dolls and stuffed animals in a semi-circle, so they were all facing me, and after singing and all the preliminaries, I began to "preach" to them. I don't know how long our "service" had been going on, but I was so engrossed in it that I didn't see a storm coming up outside. I was completely unaware until the heavy wood door behind me slammed closed with a loud thud. The noise startled me, and I ran over to try to open the door. It wouldn't budge! I pushed against it with all the might my tiny frame could muster—but still, it wouldn't move an inch. I began to cry and call for Mom, but it was of no use. I hadn't even told her where I was going when I walked past her in the kitchen. All she knew is that I was going outside to play. The wind was blowing hard, it was raining, and there was no way she could hear me calling from inside the building. I began to panic and wondered what to do.

All of a sudden, amid my distress, I heard the most reassuring sound. Princess was standing outside the outbuilding door barking for all she was worth. She barked continually until my panic-stricken mother heard her and was able to determine my whereabouts. I will never forget how happy I was to hear the door open and see Mom standing on the other side. Our loyal dog had once again risen to the challenge and been a fearless protector and friend. It seemed like she could always sense danger, and she was determined to look out for us.

When the day came that Mom and Dad made the difficult decision to give Princess away, the people we gave her to ended up giving her to the police, and she became a K9 patrol partner to one of the officers. I was very sad and cried the day she left, and we moved from the farm soon after, but I have never forgotten her.

God promised to give His angels charge over us, to keep us in all our ways. I believe His angels come to us in many different forms—some of them unlikely and often unrecognized. Hebrews 13:2 says, "Be not forgetful to entertain strangers: for thereby some have entertained angels unawares."

Princess was a protecting angel to my sister and me at the end of our lane and again that stormy day when I was so afraid. I have often wondered through the years how many other times God has sent angels to pull me and the ones I love from harm's way. And, how many times has He sent a Godly "angel" to keep me on the straight and narrow and hold me accountable in my walk with the Lord? Some are obvious. Others are not so conspicuous—perhaps they have even been strangers who slipped quietly in and out of my life with no fanfare or notice. Angels unawares, but angels nonetheless.

36

THE WALKING KING JAMES

"By faith, Abel offered unto God a more excellent sacrifice than Cain, by which he obtained witness that he was righteous, God testifying of his gifts: and by it, he being dead yet speaketh." Hebrews 11:4

Every time I hear or read this verse, I think about Papaw, my maternal grandfather. I so admire his faithful life for God and how he raised nine children, was a devoted and dedicated pastor for around 40 years, and worked a full-time 40 hour a week job in a factory simultaneously. Papaw knew the Bible more than anyone I have ever known and indisputably earned the nickname, "the walking King James." Though he has been gone for many years, "he being dead yet speaketh" encouraging me to keep pressing on for God.

My grandmother, Mimmie, passed away in late 1969, leaving Papaw a widower. A few years later, he remarried a widow from Oklahoma, where she and Papaw moved and stayed until two weeks before his death. He suffered from a physical affliction for years, and as his health continued to decline in February of 1979, he seemed to know his time was short. It was his wish to go back to his home state of Ohio and die there, specifically in Mom's home. I still remember when Mom, some of her brothers, and I made the over 800-mile trip to bring Papaw home.

When we got back to Ohio, Papaw lived exactly two weeks to the day. It was a cold, wintry Monday when Mom told me the end was near. I regret it now, but at the time, I was young and didn't want to be there when Papaw died. So I got my little neighborhood friend, Tena, from across the street, and she and I walked to the store at the end of our road. I can still remember the sinking feeling I had as we walked back home, and I saw the coroner's foreboding black car in front of our house.

A few years before Mom died, she downsized some things that were crowding her little apartment, and imagine my joy when she handed me some of the books Papaw had passed down to her and said, "Here, Cheryl. You can have these." The three I treasure most are the Bibles she gave me—two of which were Papaw's, and the other belonged to Mimmie. The Bibles are so worn that Papaw placed tape on their bindings to hold them together. When I tenderly and gently open them, I see the worn places on the sides of the pages, and I fondly remember the way he held them as he faithfully stood in front of our church every Sunday.

Once when I was attending a funeral in Ohio, my Uncle John told me he had something for me in the trunk of his car. When I got there, he handed me a treasure—another of Papaw's Bibles! This one is newer and has Papaw's name engraved in gold letters in the lower right corner of the cover.

When I opened it to look inside, I found some of Papaw's notes, and among them was a typewritten, old piece that Papaw copied from one of his favorite books, "Streams in the Desert." I include it here because this is what Papaw "the Walking King James" does to me—through my memories of him, the notes I found in his Bible, and the legacy he left behind.

"Call Back"

Author Unknown

If you have gone a little way ahead of me, call back,

'Twill cheer my heart and help my feet along the stony track;

And if, perchance, faith's light is dim, because the oil is low,

Your call will guide my lagging course as wearily I go.

Call back, and tell me He went with you into the storm,

Call back, and say He kept you when the forest roots were torn;

That, when the heavens thundered, and the earth shook the hill,

He bore you up and held you where the air was calm and still.

Oh, friend, call back and tell me for, I cannot see your face,

They say it glows with triumph now, and you have won your race;

But there are mists between us and, my spirit eyes are dim,

And I cannot see the glory though, I long for word of Him.

But if you'll say He heard you when your prayer was but a cry,

And if you'll say He saw you through, the night's sin-darkened sky;

If you have gone a little way ahead, oh friend, call back,

'Twill cheer my heart and help my feet along the stony track.

I wonder how many times Papaw felt discouraged in his work for God through the years, picked up this old piece of paper, and took comfort in thoughts of those who had already gone on before him. I can't imagine pastoring the same church for 40 years! Undoubtedly, there were moments he longed for Christians who had gone before him to "call back" and "speak" to him. He must have loved this poem to have taken the time and energy to type it out and tuck it away in his Bible.

I count the worn Bibles Mom and Uncle John gave me as some of my most cherished possessions, and I'm eternally grateful for the many hours Papaw spent in them earning his nickname. When I feel defeated and discouraged, I pick them up and hold them close to my heart and take courage in being reminded if they made it, then I can, too. How thankful I am that he, Mimmie, and my precious parents "being dead yet speak" and call back to me—words of comfort, encouragement, and a softly whispered promise that it is better farther on!

37

MY SYMBOL OF HOPE

"For I am persuaded, that neither death, nor life, nor angels, nor principalities, nor powers, nor things present, nor things to come, Nor height, nor depth, nor any other creature, shall be able to separate us from the love of God, which is in Christ Jesus our Lord." Romans 8:38,39

After going through a painful trial, my family and I took a much-needed vacation to one of my favorite places in the world—Dad's home state of Tennessee. We rented a condo just outside Pigeon Forge, with a spectacular view of the majestic Smoky Mountains. Every night would find Zach and I seated on the balcony, staring at the mountains, talking about life and the things on our minds.

Sometimes the aftermath is worse than the storm, and the repercussions are more complex than the actual blast itself. Sometimes you wake up after it is all over and wonder what just hit you and how you will ever pick up all the broken pieces and regroup and rebuild. You second-guess the choices you made and wonder if, in those split-second decisions, you did the right thing.

The enemy loves to dwell and work in the aftermath, and one of his most effective strategies, when we are struggling is to cause us to question God's love for us. "If God loved you, He would never have let this happen to you. You aren't really His child. If you were, He would have protected and shielded you from this deep hurt. God doesn't care about you. He is angry with you, and He isn't listening to your prayers. You're an outcast, and you are no longer His child. You really blew it this time." Coming to us with these kinds of thoughts, he tries to plant seeds of suspicion and doubt in our already troubled minds.

This is the state I found myself in one night on that peaceful balcony. I had gone out alone, with Zach's promise to meet me outside later. It was just me, God, the night sky, and the serene mountains across the way. Right there, amid my tranquility and gentle thoughts, nagging questions started flooding my mind. "Did we do the right thing? Was it really God Who had led us? Did we hear His voice, or was it the voice of another? Did He still care about us? Had He forsaken us? Would the hurt inside ever go away?" On and on, the questions came, each one with more intensity, and the faster they arrived, the more my anxiety increased. By the time my horrible lightning round battle with the devil eased off and subsided, I was exhausted and thoroughly discouraged.

I heard Zach opening the french doors and walking up to the chair beside me. He had barely sat down when he exclaimed, "Oh, Mama! Look!" I leaned forward to see what had caught his eye, and there, in the distance, was a huge, solid white cross, seemingly hanging in space against the night sky! We looked at each other, wondering what was holding it in place. And why hadn't we noticed it on any of the nights before?

Zach was utterly fascinated, and so was I. He didn't know anything about the war that had been waging in me, nor did he realize how tempted I was to give up on the hope that God loved us or cared about what we were going through.

As I sat there and stared at our newly discovered cross, I realized God had sent a reassuring symbol of hope at the moment I needed it most. And what better sign to send than the emblem of the suffering He endured proving the depth of His love? It was as if He were saying, "I understand. Remember the old, rugged cross? Remember *My* suffering? Remember when I cried 'Why?' to My Father? Because of what I suffered, because of what I went through, you can know with all certainty that I *do* love you, child. I love you so much that I died for you. You are not alone. I am with you. And, by the way, it **was** My voice you heard, listened to, and followed. You did the right thing. You are in the center of My perfect will for your life. Continue to follow Me. I will never leave you, and I will never forsake you."

As His peace washed over me, I stared at that cross for a long time. I never could figure out why we hadn't noticed it before, but the next day, as we were driving along, Zach and I spotted it and pointed it out to Kevin. It turned out that the ground securely supported it on the side of a mountain, and the lights of the city around it had only given the illusion that it was suspended in mid-air.

Seeing a cross is a symbol of eternal hope—a profound reminder that no matter what we go through, no matter how hard it gets, it will never be worse than what He suffered for us. If He were ever going to forsake us, He would have come down from that cross, but He stayed there and bled and died to prove the depths of His love. Nothing will ever be able to separate us from it. It will penetrate through the deepest depths of suffering and the most concrete barriers this life could ever create. Because of the love that kept Jesus on that old, rugged cross, we will ***always*** have hope.

38

BENTLEY'S REBELLION

"He, that being often reproved hardeneth his neck, shall suddenly be destroyed, and that without remedy."
Proverbs 29:1

Zach has always had a very soft spot in his heart for dogs, so when a fellow homeschool mom told me a beautiful Shih Tzu/Bichon Frise mix named Bentley needed a new home, he soon became the latest member of Zach's "pack." It didn't take us long to figure out that though Bentley was a playful, little creature, he was extremely defiant. We had a chain-link fence surrounding the two acres of our property that provided a fun, safe, free-running space for our dogs, so why any of them wanted to escape to explore the world outside was hard to understand. But Bentley was "bent" on seeing what was beyond, and he escaped out our front gate every chance he got.

You might know that most of his escapades happened when I was home alone and opened the front gate to leave. It was like a fun little game to him. He would run out the gate, stop at the end of our driveway, look at me with his big, adventurous eyes, then bolt down the road in hopes I would chase after him. I would yell his name, and he would turn around repeatedly to make sure I was following, then he would run as fast as his little legs could carry him, with me panting and gasping not too far behind! Needless to say, I tired of this "fun" pretty quickly, and each time I returned him safely home frustrated, I would make a mental promise never to do it again.

One evening, Kevin was at work, Zach had gone to spend the day with Mom, and I was home alone getting ready to leave for church. Seeing yet another grand opportunity for freedom, Bentley bolted out the gate when I opened it, and I watched as he reached the end of our driveway, turned, cocked his cute, little head, and looked at me as if to say, "Come on, chase me, it's playtime!"

I started to run after him and play along, but having only a short time to pick up Zach and Mom and make it to church on time, I turned to get in the car. After all, I reasoned, how many times had this happened? I left, hoping he would do the right thing, come back on his own, and wiggle his way under the gate as he had in the past.

When Zach and I returned from church that night, all the dogs came to greet us at the gate—all of them, that is, except Bentley. This time, he was nowhere to be seen. Zach began to look for him, and there beside our mailbox by the street, laid a furry, little, black heap. Bentley had rebelled one too many times. By the direction he was headed, it appeared he was on his way back home to try to squeeze back inside the gate. This time he didn't make it—this time, his wild disobedience cost him his life.

Whenever I think about Bentley and the wrong choice he

made, I am reminded of free will. I could have run after him, finally overtaken him, and forced him, kicking and squealing, to come back home. But that time, I left the choice to him and let him go.

Free will is a powerful yet powerfully dangerous force. God has given each of us a mind of our own and the freedom to choose. He wants us to serve Him because we want to—because we love Him. He is "not willing that any should perish, but that all should come to repentance." (II Peter 3:9) He paid a heavy price to make a way for us to live with Him throughout eternity, but He will not force His way upon any of us. Ultimately, the choice is left to you and me.

Have you made the wrong choice? Are you headed in the wrong direction? No matter how many reckless spiritual chances you have taken or how many times you have rebelled and wandered outside the parameters of our Father's will, the unconditional love in His heart for you remains. He waits with open arms. He wants you to come home.

39

THE BROKEN ONES

"The LORD is nigh unto them that are of a broken heart; and saveth such as be of a contrite spirit."
Psalm 34:18

As we stood in line at the grocery store and I reached for the divider to separate our groceries from the customer's purchases in front of us, I observed that the only "groceries" he was buying were four cases of beer. He had left the line to get cigarettes from the customer service desk, and when he walked back, I noticed the pitiful, shabby condition of his shoes and clothes. His thin, haggard appearance showed that he needed a good, home-cooked meal, and his hands shook so badly he could hardly endorse the government check the cashier handed back to him to sign. It occurred to me that the man wasn't buying any food at all —nothing, not even a loaf of bread. Just four cases of beer, and I couldn't see how many cartons of cigarettes.

How does he survive on alcohol and nicotine alone? Is that

possible? After the cashier deducted his purchases from his government check, she handed him back a little over $300.00. Would that amount need to stretch the rest of the entire month? How long would it take him to drink the four cases of beer? Would he buy more with the remaining money? How would he pay rent, utilities, and other living expenses from such a meager amount? I thought of his shoes and torn clothing and mentally calculated how far the amount of his purchase could have gone in buying nutritious food and necessities. Is there anyone anywhere who loves him and cares about what happens to him?

These were the questions going through my mind as I tried my best to make eye contact with the man in front of me. I so wanted to give him a friendly smile and speak a few kind words, but the entire time he stood there, he either looked down or around—anywhere except in my direction, almost as if he were ashamed. If only he knew that I know the truth—he and I are not all that different.

As I watched him put the last of the four cases of beer and the bag of cigarettes in his otherwise empty cart, tears came to my eyes, and I breathed a silent prayer for him.

Not one of us is exempt from addictions, bad choices, and destructive habits. None of us is better than the other simply because we do the right things. The imperfect, judgmental churchgoer sitting in a pew every Sunday is no more pious than the drug addict lying in the street. The truth is, we are all broken, and but for God's grace, we would all be lost for eternity.

When I was little, Mom and Dad bought me a beautiful "walking" doll that I named Marcia. Other than the many joyful hours of "playing house" with Marcia, the thing I remember most about her was that her right leg often fell off when she "walked." Every time it did, I panicked because I didn't know how to fix it. So, I would run to my Daddy with my broken doll, and he would stop whatever he was doing because, to me, it was an emergency, and Marcia needed her leg! In my eyes, Dad was a miracle worker, and it took a long time for me to figure out that all he had to do to make Marcia good as new again was to reattach a rubber band inside the top of her leg. Dad would hand Marcia back to me, and off I would go, smiling and happy that my beloved doll could walk again. What was so impossible for me to fix was so easy for Dad.

Just as my Daddy would drop everything to fix my broken toy, nothing is more important to God, our Heavenly Father, than to fix our broken lives. I have thought of the man in the grocery store and wondered about him from time to time. I hope someone told him that no matter how messed up our lives become or how far beyond repair they appear to be, God knows just what to do to fix every bit of our brokenness. ***All we have to do is bring Him all the pieces.***

40

ANGELS & SLEEPY DRIVERS

"Yet a little sleep, a little slumber, a little folding of the hands to sleep: so shall thy poverty come as one that travelleth, and thy want as an armed man."
Proverbs 6:10,11

It makes me very sleepy to drive. I get under the wheel, become very relaxed, and before I know it, drowsiness takes over. I have prayed many prayers during road trips as Kevin and Zach slept while I drove, and I realized that both of their lives were in my hands. What if I failed? What if I gave in to the strong temptation to close my eyes—even just for an instant? Then what?

Years ago, when my Uncle Donnie lived in California, he drove on a narrow two-lane road with 20-30 foot drop-offs on both sides and no guard rails. He became very sleepy, and the next thing he knew, he woke up to find that his car was on a bridge scraping the railing in the left-hand lane! What kept him from veering off the road before making it to the bridge with railings? What kept another car from hitting him head-on while he was driving in the wrong lane?

Psalm 34:7 says, "The angel of the LORD encampeth round about them that fear him, and delivereth them." And Psalm 91:11 says, "For He shall give His angels charge over thee, to keep thee in all thy ways." We could all tell stories about times we "just missed" an accident or made other narrow escapes. The only explanation for our survival was that there had to be protecting angels—encamping round about us, standing between us and danger, shielding us, directing us, and getting our attention just in time. There are probably more scenarios of God's divine intervention that we do not know about than the ones we do.

Just as Kevin and Zach trust me to stay awake when it is my turn to drive, there are those in each of our lives who depend on us to keep awake spiritually. Someone is counting on us to remain diligent about our walk with the Lord, and they need to know that we won't drop the ball or fall asleep on the job. We may think they don't notice and feel that our role to remain watchful and prayerful is inconsequential, but we couldn't be more wrong.

Kevin's Dad was a World War II veteran, and he used to tell of the time he was assigned to guard the trash. Even though it seemed like a useless waste of time and was such a dull, sleep-inducing job, others depended on him to faithfully watch. He must have become very sleepy. What if he had nodded off? What if there had been an enemy hiding in the trash waiting for him to let down his guard and fall asleep? What would have become of the other soldiers who were counting on him to stay awake?

When Jesus went to the Garden of Gethsemane on the night that would forever change the world, He realized what was riding on His faithfulness. He took Peter, James, and John with Him, longing for their prayers and watchful support. After praying the most anguished prayer in history, Matthew 26:40-43 says, "And He cometh unto the disciples, and findeth them asleep, and saith unto Peter, 'What, could ye not watch with me one hour? Watch and pray that ye enter not into temptation: the spirit indeed *is* willing, but the flesh *is* weak.' He went away again the second time and prayed, saying, 'O My Father, if this cup may not pass away from Me, except I drink it, Thy will be done.' And He came and found them asleep again: for their eyes were heavy."

Jesus came to His disciples hoping to find them alert and repeatedly found them sleeping when He needed them most.

Sometimes we feel our labors are in vain, and we should slack off. We are tempted to miss a few days of prayer and Bible reading and give in to the lackadaisical spiritual sleepiness and lethargy of our time, but if we fail to guard our post of duty carefully, how will it affect the ones who depend on us most? Who is counting on our faithfulness?

Galatians 6:9 says, "And let us not be weary in well doing: for in due season we shall reap if we faint not." Just as it just isn't worth even one wink of sleep under the wheel while driving, it is not worth one moment of spiritual neglect. ***Far too much is at stake.***

41

THE PAINTING

"Delight thyself also in the LORD, and he shall give thee the desires of thine heart." Psalm 37:4

While shopping in a gift shop with Kevin and Zach, my eyes were almost immediately drawn to a beautiful painting on the wall. The setting appeared to be an inside room of a large, old, southern mansion. A young lady stood in front of an open glass door with her back turned, looking out over a pond in the spacious, sprawling backyard. In her hand was a letter, and because you could not see her face or expression, you were left to imagine what the words in the letter conveyed. Maybe it was news from her beloved or a letter of goodbye or some sort of invitation that required her to make a decision. Something about her demeanor was nostalgic and made me feel a bit melancholy, as if the letter contained pensive or contemplative news.

I called for Kevin to come to look, and he agreed that it was beautiful. He tried his best to convince me to buy and take it home

—it is rare that something catches my eye and captures my heart the way this painting did—*I felt so drawn to it*. As tempted as I was, the price tag convinced me that it was an extravagant and unnecessary expense. I lingered and admired it for a while, and then when Kevin and Zach were ready, we left the store.

I thought about it from time to time, especially while driving past the shop, and I wondered if it had sold. It was something I wished for but felt would always be out of reach. I could certainly live without it, but I kept daydreaming about how beautiful it would look hanging on our bedroom wall.

One day, Zach and I drove to the town where the gift shop was located, and having other things to tend to, the painting was the last thing on my mind. Right before we got into the central part of town, I looked ahead and saw a yard sale, and as we were passing by, I could hardly believe my eyes! There, propped up against some kind of crate or box at the edge of the sale, was the painting! It was as if God had prompted them to place it near the road, where I couldn't help seeing it.

I hurriedly turned around, drove back to the sale, and Zach and I got out of the car. Expecting the worst, I mustered the nerve to ask the gentleman how much he wanted for the painting. I heard the word seven, and my heart sunk as I thought he would say $75.00. Then I heard him say $7.00! In disbelief, I repeated, "Seven dollars?" He nodded his head, and I could hardly believe it! Seven dollars. There it was, within my grasp after all, in its beautiful, gold-colored, Victorian-looking frame. I paid the man, and Zach and I were on our way to finish running errands so that we could hurry home. After wishing for the painting for so long, I knew just where I wanted to hang it—on our bedroom wall right next to my side of the bed.

I find a sense of peace and curious comfort each time I look at the painting. I am drawn in by the grandeur of the mansion, lovely antique furnishings, beautiful woodwork, crown molding near the ceilings, swans swimming in the pond outside the glass door, and of course, the mystery of the lady holding the letter behind her back. All of it takes me away to a place I will only ever travel in my imagination, but that is enough.

God cares about all that touches our lives, even those little things in life that make us happy. Even though I didn't need the painting, my longing for it did not escape Him. I will never understand how it ended up in the hands of someone who included it in a yard sale by the side of the same road we traveled that day. And I will probably never figure out how He orchestrated a way for me to have something that seemed so far beyond my grasp. He has promised to supply our every need, and He faithfully does, but, oh, so often, He goes far behind that and gives us the desires of our hearts, too.

42

PASS IT ON

"I have shewed you all things, how that so laboring ye ought to support the weak, and to remember the words of the Lord Jesus, how He said, 'It is more blessed to give than to receive.'" Acts 20:35

Anonymous giving that seeks no accolades or recognition comes from the heart and is what true charity is all about.

When Zach was a baby, he, Mom, and I enjoyed a meal in a local diner, and during the meal, we noticed an older couple sitting across from us. Now and then, our eyes met, and we exchanged smiles, but they finished eating before us and left the restaurant without our sharing any verbal communication. It was what happened next that spoke volumes. Without fanfare or our noticing, they walked to the counter and discreetly bought our meal. Imagine our surprise when we finished eating, tried to pay the tab, and the cashier told us they had already paid! Their generosity deeply touched our hearts.

Not long after, Mom, Zach, and I ate lunch at another local restaurant and were seated at a table adjacent to a gentleman dressed in a business suit. There were no words exchanged between us, just one quick smile when he looked our way. After he quietly finished his meal and left, our waiter brought our check to us, and it showed a zero balance! We asked her why, and she told us it had been paid in full by the thoughtful man who sat next to us.

Another time, Zach and I were shopping in a Christian bookstore, where he spotted the latest Veggie Tales DVD for sale. It was his favorite show, and I knew how much it meant to him when he asked if he could have it. Funds were limited, and oh, how it broke my heart to tell him no! He sweetly accepted my answer without complaint, and we made our way to the front of the store. Not realizing anyone noticed our conversation in the toy aisle, I was shocked to hear a lady in the line next to us say, "Ma'am, would you allow me to bless your little boy with that DVD?" I was nearly moved to tears and asked her if she was sure. She beamed as she nodded her head, paid for the DVD, and handed it to Zach. We could not have been more grateful.

Each of our benefactors performed a much-appreciated random act of kindness, then were on their way, never to be seen by us again. I regret not being able to repay them personally for their benevolence, but I can do something to perpetuate their giving spirit. I can pass along their goodwill to others, and in doing so, I have learned one thing. As much as I have loved, appreciated, and enjoyed receiving many kindnesses through the years, I receive an even bigger blessing when I am the one who is doing the giving.

Acts 10:38 says, "How God anointed Jesus of Nazareth with the Holy Ghost and with power: Who went about doing good and healing all that were oppressed of the devil; for God was with Him." Jesus never wasted precious time or missed a golden opportunity to help another. In Matthew 25:40, He said, "Verily I say unto you, 'Inasmuch as ye have done it unto one of the least of these My brethren, ye have done it unto Me.'" Who wouldn't want to buy Jesus a meal? Who wouldn't give anything for the opportunity to pay for something He needs?

Proverbs 3:27 says, "Withhold not good from them to whom it is due when it is in the power of thine hand to do it." Sometimes we are just not in tune with the needs of others around us. Sometimes we are so burdened with our own problems that we forget there are those in worse circumstances. It is amazing how doing something nice for someone else inevitably causes us to feel better about our own situation.

One day, as I shopped for groceries, an opportunity to "pass it on" was presented. I noticed a grandmotherly-looking woman with a baby in tow standing in the baby aisle, staring at diapers. She finally ended up picking up a pack of the off-brand and walked past me, mumbling something about being down to her last $10.00. As she did, the Holy Spirit began to remind me that I had a little extra money in my wallet.

By God's providence, I ended up in line right behind her. I noticed that all she was buying were the diapers and a pack of peanut butter and crackers. Compassion overpowered the awkwardness I felt, and I mustered the courage to say, "Ma'am, would you allow me to bless you?" She looked at me cautiously, at first. Then with a little more coaxing, she consented, took her two meager items, along with her $10.00 bill, thanked me, and left the store. Gratitude was written all over her face, but let me assure you that her blessing could not have been greater than mine.

Imagine our world if each one of us would do one random act of kindness every single day. It doesn't always have to be monetary. Think of all the ways others have blessed you, then purpose it in your heart, starting today, to pass it on.

43

THE BENEFITS OF WAITING

"Wait on the Lord: be of good courage, and He shall strengthen thine heart: wait, I say on the Lord."
Psalm 27:14

Zach has always loved Christmas. To this day, his enthusiasm over the wonder of the season is contagious, and seeing it all through his eyes, makes me appreciate it even more. He loves it so much that we start preparing for it early at our house—decorating, shopping, planning our baking, and making homemade gifts. The fact that we start so early allows us to enjoy it longer, but it also makes it harder for Zach to wait!

Every night before he goes to bed, he checks off another day on the calendar and says, "Mama, just ___ more days!" and as he stares at his pile of gifts each day, he says he doesn't know how he'll wait until Christmas. He was born on December 26th, which makes Christmas even more special to him and the wait even more unbearable—he waits all year long for his two favorite days of all.

I don't suppose anyone enjoys the process of waiting. Time spent waiting seems wasted, but Psalm 27:14 tells us that during times of waiting, the Lord strengthens our heart, and Isaiah 40:31 says, "But they that wait upon the Lord shall renew their strength; they shall mount up with wings as eagles; they shall run, and not be weary, and they shall walk, and not faint."

One of the hardest parts of waiting on the Lord is that the wait time is indefinite—God doesn't give us the expiration date of our waiting. If He did, we would have a visible goal to work toward, like Zach counting down the days to Christmas. Knowing he is one day closer to his goal each day encourages him that he has one less day to wait.

I will never forget a comment one of my co-workers made when she saw Zach for the first time, shortly after he was born. She knew Kevin and I had waited 12 ½ years for a child of our own, and upon seeing Zach, she commented on how precious he was, then turned to me and said, "Cheryl, wouldn't it have been a lot easier to wait if you knew you had *this* to look forward to?" I thought back over all of those long years of waiting, realizing she was so right. Had I been able to look ahead and see the baby God would one day place in our arms, it would have made all those years of waiting seem easier to endure.

Just as we do not know how long our trials will last, none of us know the expiration date of our lives or how long we will have to wait for Jesus to come back. He told His disciples shortly before He ascended in Acts 1:7, "It is not for you to know the times or the seasons, which the Father hath put in His own power." What we do know, however, is that our earthly lives will one day end—

either by death or by the coming of Jesus Christ, whichever comes first.

When Jesus was preparing His disciples for His departure from earth, He told them in John 14:2, "In my Father's house are many mansions: if *it were* not *so*, I would have told you. I go to prepare a place for you." And what a place it will be! I Corinthians 2:9 says, "But as it is written, 'Eye hath not seen, nor ear heard, neither have entered into the heart of man, the things which God hath prepared for them that love him.'" In verse 3 of John 14, Jesus went on to tell His disciples that He would come again and receive them unto Himself, "that where I am, ye may be also." That is a promise!

With the resources we have, we do our best to make Zach's Christmas as special as it can be each year. We hope that when he sees the gifts we've bought for him, he will feel that it was worth the "trial" he went through to wait to open them. Even though he hasn't opened his presents, he has faith to believe that the neatly wrapped packages beneath our tree are not empty. He has the hope to believe that if he waits, he will find gifts inside.

We haven't seen Heaven, but in our hearts, we have faith to believe it is real. If we could interview those who have arrived at that beautiful place ahead of us, they would all agree that it is very real and most definitely worth the wait!

Sometimes life can be trying and even become a burden. Trials beset us on every hand, and we begin to wonder if it is worthwhile to keep pressing forward. In challenging circumstances, it is easy to forget that God has something extraordinary in store for all of us, and this life, with all its problems, tests, and tribulations, is simply a place to wait until He calls us home. Hebrews 10:35 says, "Cast not away, therefore, your confidence, which hath great recompence of reward."

One day the waiting will be over, and we will find that the benefits of Heaven far surpass the troubles of this life.

44

AND PETER

*"But go your way, tell His disciples **and Peter** that He goeth before you into Galilee: there shall ye see Him, as He said unto you." Mark 16:7 (Emphasis mine)*

*P*eter—if there was ever a disciple I feel like I can relate to, he's the one. Strong-willed, too quick to speak, the first to want to "do" something to fix things, fiercely loyal, yet falling short when it matters most. He occupied one of the places in Jesus' inner circle—one of the intimate three invited into pivotal parts of His ministry, while others were kept at a distance.

It was Peter who vowed that no matter who else forsook Him, Jesus could always count on him—even if it cost his life. Just a few hours later, he had broken that vow, vehemently denied being Jesus' disciple, and even went so far as to curse and swear that he did not know Him. Jesus had warned Peter this would happen, and as the cruel Roman soldiers led Jesus past him, "Peter remembered the word of Jesus, which said unto him, 'Before the cock crow, thou shalt deny Me thrice.' And he went out and wept bitterly." Matthew 26:75

How he must have wished he could go back and do things over! He had let Him down severely, and now, nothing he could ever say or do could take it back or make it right. So, he went out and wept bitter tears, wrenched from a broken spirit and a contrite heart.

Moments like these are some of the lowest possible points of the human condition. Only those who have passed through such mournful valleys of failure can relate and understand. And moments like these are places of redemption, forgiveness, and restoration—catalysts of transformation to walk away from and never be the same.

On Resurrection Morning, the angel met Mary at the empty tomb of Jesus and said, "But go your way, tell His disciples **and Peter** that He goeth before you into Galilee." The angel did not just say, "tell His disciples." Peter was a disciple and could undoubtedly have been included in the same group as the others, but the angel's message was clear, "tell His disciples **and Peter**." Oh, the meaning in those two little words!

I can only imagine the tortured mental anguish Peter suffered from the time of the crucifixion to the moment Mary came to him bearing a personalized message from the angel. Then to feel the enormous relief hearing Jesus was waiting for **him** in Galilee! The invitation was accompanied by no mention of scorn, scolding, or "I told you so, Peter!" Instead, when Jesus saw His disciples for the first time after His resurrection, the first word He spoke was, "Peace." John 20:19 Complete reconciliation, as if Peter had never denied Him at all.

In Luke 7:36-50, we find the account of a "sinner" who washed

Jesus' feet with her tears, kissed them, anointed them with oil, and dried them with her hair. When the owner of the house secretly found fault with Jesus allowing such a sinful woman to touch Him, Jesus said, "'There was a certain creditor which had two debtors: the one owed five hundred pence, and the other fifty. And when they had nothing to pay, he frankly forgave them both. Tell me, therefore, which of them will love him most?' Simon answered and said, 'I suppose that *he*, to whom he forgave most.' And He said unto him, 'Thou hast rightly judged. Wherefore I say unto thee, her sins, which are many, are forgiven; for she loved much: but to whom little is forgiven, *the same* loveth little."

Peter was forgiven much, and because of the unconditional, all-encompassing forgiveness Jesus extended to Peter, he was able to write these words, "The Lord is not slack concerning His promise, as some men count slackness; but is longsuffering to us-ward, not willing that any should perish, but that all should come to repentance." 2 Peter 3:9

Peter knew firsthand how it felt to fail Jesus on a monumental level when Jesus needed him most, then be offered complete, undeserved forgiveness. As a result of that, the measure of love Peter had for Him from that moment forward was the profound driving force of his life. Nothing demonstrates this more than what happened in the moments leading up to his death.

Tradition teaches us that Peter was sentenced to death by Nero, and just before he died, he was forced by the Romans to watch his wife's crucifixion.

"They say, accordingly, that the blessed Peter, on seeing his wife led to death, rejoiced on account of her call and conveyance home and called very encouragingly and comfortingly, addressing her by name, "Remember thou the Lord." *Written by Clement of Alexandria in "The Stromata, or Miscellanies: Book VII."*

When it came Peter's time, he asked to be crucified upside down because he did not feel worthy to die in the same way as Jesus.

Nehemiah 9:17 says, "But thou *art* a God ready to pardon, gracious and merciful, slow to anger, and of great kindness."

"***And Peter.***" And you. Thank God, and me, too.

45

NO JUNK

"And God saw everything that He had made, and, behold, it was very good." Genesis 1:31

When I was little, Dad brought a plaque home to me. It had a picture of a child with its chubby face propped on pudgy elbows, and it said, "I must be special, 'cause God don't make no junk." I put it in my room and cherished it because Dad gave it to me, but as I read it often, I also came to thoroughly believe its message.

Oh, for the innocent hopefulness of childhood when life is simple and truth is readily embraced! My parents loved me, thought I was special, taught me that God loved me, too, and I believed them with all my heart.

As a child, we accept without suspicion what we are told and taught, whether the input is positive or negative. As grownups, we question the affirmations and positive truths, and we struggle to disbelieve the damaging lies and stigmas attached to us as children.

In the first chapter of Genesis, we find the complete account of the creation of our world and everything in it. During each of the six days of creation, God surveyed His workmanship, and repeatedly, time after time, God "saw that it was good."

God doesn't "make no junk." Every child should hear that. Careless remarks made by parents leave deep, lifelong impressions on their children and shape their self-worth. Comments like "This is the baby of the family—he was a mistake," or "This is our middle child—she will never amount to much" are death blows to a child's self-esteem. They are not only detrimental in the moment they are spoken, but the wounds inflicted turn into ugly scars that haunt a person their entire life. Should any of God's creations ever be described as an accident or worthless?

For years I have tried to affirm the value of someone who was constantly degraded as a child. The grown-up person I dearly love and deeply admire struggles to believe me when I say how proud I am of them, how special they are, and what great things they have accomplished and have yet to conquer. Every compliment is quickly dismissed and replaced by the mention of flaws and discrepancies. I don't know if they will ever truly see the beautiful creation they are, or believe how much I love them, or ever think they are worth anything at all.

Sadly, we measure our worth by things such as other people's opinions of us, labels that were pinned on us as children, our weight, complexion, hair, body shape, education, the happiness and stability of our marriage, our job, and how much money we have accumulated. God doesn't see us that way at all. His eye of love was on us long before we were even conceived!

"Before I formed thee in the belly, I knew thee, and before

thou camest forth out of the womb, I sanctified thee, *and* I ordained thee a prophet unto the nations." Jeremiah 1:5

When the prophet Samuel searched for the next king of Israel, God sent Him to Jesse's house and told him one of Jesse's sons would be king. When Samuel saw Jesse's son, Eliab, he said, "Surely the Lord's anointed is before him." Whatever the reason for Samuel's assumption, Eliab was not God's choice. I Samuel 16:7 says, "But the Lord said unto Samuel, 'Look not on his countenance, or on the height of his stature; because I have refused him: for the Lord seeth not as man seeth; for man looketh on the outward appearance, but the Lord looketh on the heart.'" Jesse brought in several more of his sons for Samuel to consider, but no matter how they looked on the outside, they were not the chosen one.

Finally, Samuel asked if Jesse had any more sons, and as an afterthought, his youngest son, David, was brought in before Samuel. Evidently, no one thought David should even be a contender—he was Jesse's youngest son, and his lowly job was to keep the sheep. Who would have thought he was worthy of being king? But, God didn't see David as others saw him. Acts 13:22 tells us that David was a man after God's own heart. When David was brought before Samuel, the Lord said, "Arise, anoint him: for this is he."

Do you feel like an afterthought? A mistake? Whatever you may have been led to believe, you are no accident. Your life didn't "just happen" or "come along at the wrong time" or whatever other lies you may have heard. You are valuable. You have great worth in the sight of God. When He created you, He surveyed His creation, and "He saw that it was very good." He doesn't look at you through human eyes, nor does He compare you to others, no matter what they look like on the outside or how "together" they appear to be.

Like Esther, you are here "for such a time as this." Esther 4:14. God created you for this place and time, and "You must be special, 'cause God don't make no junk."

46

THE LORD REMEMBERS

"He maketh the barren woman to keep house and to be a joyful mother of children. Praise ye the Lord." Psalm 113:9

When Kevin and I were married in June of 1988, we assumed having children would be the next logical step in our lives. It never occurred to us that God's plan may be different from our assumptions, but it soon became apparent that having children would not be our next step and possibly never a part of our story at all.

In late 1991, during a time of one of Dad's severe health crises, I found myself stretched on the floor one night, in earnest prayer for him. As my tears fell and hit the floor, I unexpectedly heard the still, small voice of the Lord whispering a promise to let me know that Kevin and I would indeed have a child of our own one day. Even though I was praying for Dad, not petitioning the Lord for a baby, being given that promise to cling to during such a dark time brought an immeasurable sense of comfort.

Over the next several years, that precious promise was put to the test as time went by, with absolutely no sign of it being fulfilled. The story of Hannah found in I Samuel 1:1-28 became my mainstay, along with the stories of Sarah, Rebekkah, Rachel, Manoah's wife, and Elizabeth, all of whom had barren wombs that were healed and miraculously opened by God for a divine purpose. Hannah became the mother of Samuel; Sarah became the mother of Isaac; Rebekkah became the mother of twins, Jacob and Esau; Rachel became the mother of Joseph; Manoah's wife became the mother of Samson; Elizabeth became the mother of John the Baptist. It struck me that each of these six women's infertility journeys ended with the birth of a son who was mightily used by God. Romans 4:13-21 came alive to me, especially this in verse 17, "*even* God, who quickeneth the dead, and calleth those things which be not as though they were," and this in verse 18, "who against hope believed in hope," and this in verses 19-21, "And being not weak in faith, he considered not his own body now dead, when he was about an hundred years old, neither yet the deadness of Sara's womb: he staggered not at the promise of God through unbelief; but was strong in faith, giving glory to God; and being fully persuaded that, what He had promised, He was able also to perform."

After going to doctors and through medical testing, I finally received a diagnosis that explained my own "barrenness." We were given the option of taking fertility treatments with the understanding that even if we did, my chances of conceiving a child were very slim. We prayed and decided that we would decline treatments and place it all in God's hands, trusting His will to direct the outcome.

Hearing a doctor attach a medical term to our infertility struggles intensified the testing of my faith. Though I had been taught all my life that God faithfully keeps His promises, by this time, Kevin and I had been married for almost ten years, and I felt He had forgotten, changed His mind, or I hadn't really heard His voice. The thing I failed to see was when God makes a promise, He does not include the word "immediately." There is almost always a pause in the waiting room before we see the promise fulfilled, and just because He has not yet delivered on His promise does not mean He won't. The truth is, He is not on our timetable, nor is He boxed into our whims and wishes and demands, but He never makes a promise that He doesn't keep.

Charles Spurgeon said, "God has given no pledge that He will not redeem and encouraged no hope that He will not fulfill."

When we don't understand His logic, we must trust His wisdom in doing things according to His divine order and timing.

I Samuel 1:19,20 says, "And they rose up in the morning early, and worshipped before the Lord, and returned, and came to their house to Ramah: and Elkanah knew Hannah his wife, **and the Lord remembered her**. Wherefore it came to pass when the time was come about after Hannah had conceived, that she bare a son, and called his name Samuel, *saying*, 'Because I have asked him of the Lord.'"

Twelve and a half years after we were married and over nine years after God made that promise, **He also remembered us** when He sent Kevin and me the desire of our hearts—a son, whom we named Zachary. Our waiting had felt like an eternity, but I have often thought of the fact that our time in the waiting room was exactly half the time Abraham and Sarah had to wait for their son, Isaac. Though I had pushed God's promise far to the back of my mind and thought He forgot, it was as fresh to Him as the night He made it. **The Lord remembered**, and confirmation came in such a sweet, unexpected way.

Early in my pregnancy, we began discussing baby names and decided right off if our baby was a girl, her name would be Hannah (of course!), but we were struggling to decide on a boy's name. As we left the doctor's office the day it was confirmed our baby was a boy, Kevin turned to me and said, "I like the name Zachary—I'd like to call him Zach." I instantly liked it, too, and we never looked back.

A few years after Zach was born, I was in a Christian bookstore looking at the little cards that show the meanings of names. Of course, I looked for" Zachary," and when I found it, I stood there speechless, in complete awe of God, His promises, His purpose, and His faithfulness. The name Zachary literally means "The Lord remembers." I could hardly believe my eyes. Neither Kevin nor I ever thought to investigate the meaning of the name "Zachary," but God knew when He placed a love for that name in Kevin's heart and prompted him to mention it to me that day in our doctor's parking lot.

The Lord does remember. Even when I doubted and thought He had long forgotten—the Lord remembered. And His timing was perfect.

47

THE STRENGTH OF HORSES

"A horse is a vain thing for safety: neither shall he deliver any by his great strength." Psalm 33:17

Ever since I was young, I have been fascinated with horses. Even though I've only ridden a horse one time, have never personally owned one, and found the vastness of their size intimidating when I used to visit them at my Uncle Cecil's boarding stable, I find them to be one of the most majestic, noble animals God ever created. There is just something comforting about watching them run free and uninhibited. They are spirited and proud, and incredibly strong.

But, with all its strength and nobility, a horse is powerless to keep anyone safe. It would be vain to depend on it for protection, and it could never be counted on to deliver anyone by its great strength. Many a rider in battle has lost their life while riding on the back of a horse. Even though it is beautiful to look at, exhilarating to ride, and powerful to pull loads, it could never shield anyone from danger.

There are many things in this life in which we can put our trust. *Money* makes people feel safe and comforted, and knowing they have a nest egg to fall back on gives a certain sense of security and peace. But, what if the money is spent? What if the investments don't pay off? What if the economy crumbles, and all is lost? Psalm 62:10 says, "If riches increase, set not your heart *upon them*." And Proverbs 23:5 says, "Wilt thou set thine eyes upon that which is not? For *riches* certainly make themselves wings; they fly away as an eagle toward Heaven." Many who have placed their trust in money have ended up taking their own lives when their source of security was taken away.

During my career in banking, I worked in areas of considerable wealth along the "Treasure Coast" of Florida. I never ceased to be amazed over the emphasis people placed on money and the extremes to which they were willing to go to keep it safe and protected. Proverbs 27:24 says, "For riches *are* not forever: and doth the crown *endure* to every generation?" In the end, it matters not how much wealth we accumulate. When life is over, we will have no choice but to leave it all behind.

Many times we seek a *person* to be our deliverer and source of safety. But, even though those who hold our best interests close to their hearts are mortal, with limited power. However much they want to be, they cannot be our savior.

Some delve passionately into their *career*, seeking promotion and prestige. They spend years preparing for it, assuming once they have the title and accomplish their long-term goals, they will be happy, and life will be perfect. But what about the day the boss comes around to say things aren't going as well as expected, and the termination date is set? What about the moment the news comes to us that someone else got the promotion, even though we gave it all we had?

Chasing after the things of this world is like a racing horse trying to reach the dangled carrot in front of him. It just never quite happens, does it? The brass ring is always slightly out of reach—even after we've attained our carefully set goals and ambitions. When all is quiet, and we must face ourselves in the stillness, the emptiness remains. We find that the big house, bank account, prestigious career, extra-marital relationship, title next to our name, our spouse, our children, all the horses in the world—none of these can deliver, satisfy, or make us complete. At the end of the day, there is a gaping hole in each person that only God can fill.

After everything he had accomplished, Solomon, one of the wisest men who ever lived, said this near the end of the book of Ecclesiastes, "Let us hear the conclusion of the whole matter: fear God, and keep His commandments: for this *is* the whole *duty* of man." Ecclesiastes 12:13 If you read this deep, insightful book, you will see that with all of his wealth and riches and sources of security, he still felt and recognized the vanity and void left by worldly things. Only God could bring about the peace his soul craved.

I think his father, David, had learned the same secret when he said, "Some *trust* in chariots, and some in horses: but we will remember the name of the LORD our God." Psalm 20:7

He is truly our only hope.

48

TOGETHER

"God setteth the solitary in families." Psalm 68:6

When Zach was little and had a tummy ache, I could usually identify pretty quickly whether it came from feeling anxious or troubled over something. I learned that what helped him most during those times was comfort and addressing his emotional needs, so we used to play a little game. We took journeys, in our imaginations, of course, to places we like to go. We revisited vacation spots and pretended we were there, enjoying all of our favorite things again.

During one early-morning episode, he woke me up feeling very bad, so together, we walked to the living room, and through sleepy eyes, I took him on an imaginary one-month-long expedition. We encompassed five states and went to some exciting and fascinating places. Shortly after our "trip," Zach felt all better and ready to go back to bed. After I tucked him back safely in and kissed his cheek, he said, "Wherever we are together, I'm happy."

I walked away and thought about what he had just said. Out of the mouth of babes! As I pondered on his simple statement, I came to the full realization that he was 100% right. Togetherness, with the ones we love most, makes all of us happy. The component of moral support, surrounded by love and those who love us, is invaluable. Through the years, some of the darkest times of my life were softened and made tolerable just by Kevin's touch, of having him near, and of looking across the room and seeing Zach and knowing he is okay and with us. Just having them near me brings a sense of confirmation and assurance that all will ultimately be well as long as we are together.

Together. It is important. It is essential to a life well-lived. Even our dear Lord needed that togetherness and the moral support of knowing the ones He loved most were near to Him. I wonder if some of the sadness and heartbreak He experienced in the Garden of Gethsemane might have been because He would soon have to leave His dearest friends. He was also keenly aware of the loneliness and desolation they would feel from the horrible loss of no longer having Him near to lead, comfort, and guide their every move.

Remember how His heart went out to His mother when He was hanging on the cross? "When Jesus, therefore, saw His mother and the disciple standing by, whom He loved, He saith unto His mother, 'Woman, behold thy son!' Then saith He to the disciple, 'Behold thy mother!' And from that hour, that disciple took her unto his own home." John 19:26,27

Jesus knew her mother-heart was breaking with the overwhelming sense of losing Him. He knew she would need comfort and care after His departure, so in His dying agony, He made provisions for her to have someone to live with and who would make "together" a possibility for her.

Family matters. Regardless of how imperfect they are, how short they fall from someone else's "perfect family" ideal, or how big or small they may be, you are abundantly blessed if you have a family. To have someone who worries when you aren't home on time, someone to call and share the good news with, and someone who has your back no matter what—these are blessings more precious than gold.

It matters not how many earthly treasures we accumulate. They can't comfort us or care about us or respond to our needs. What matters are the people who make "together" real for us. As Zach so accurately pointed out, happiness comes from being with the ones we love—no matter where we are.

49

KEEPING LOVE ALIVE

"But from the beginning of the creation, God made them male and female. For this cause shall a man leave his father and mother, and cleave to his wife; and they twain shall be one flesh: so then they are no more twain, but one flesh. What therefore God hath joined together, let not man put asunder." Mark 10:6-9

There is tremendous happiness and a deeply gratifying sense of security and comfort that comes from keeping marriage vows and loving the same person over a lifetime. The longer two people are together, the more one they become as joint history is built through laughter, tears, and the makings of everyday life.

Spring of life has faded, and Kevin and I are now approaching that season between the end of summer and the dawning of autumn—where we are no longer referred to as "the young couple," but "middle-aged." How did we get here so fast? In my mind, we are still young, full of zest and hope for our *future*, while reality reveals that what started as hopeful excitement is now permanently written on the pages of the history book of our *past*.

Honeymoon emotions fade. Life sets in. Bills, aging and death of parents, growing families, health issues, and uncertain futures become stark reality. Time marches on. So, how do we keep love alive? How do we maintain a lifetime of faithfulness in the face of a culture that inflicts non-stop temptation? How do we retain that initial tenderness and deep emotion? How do we reinforce the ties that bind while everything around us suggests giving up the fight?

When Kevin and I are asked the secret to the longevity of our marriage, our answer always boils down to the fact that we can take zero credit—all glory and gratitude to the One who brought us together—and these three main points.

Marriage takes three—God, Kevin, and me.

God must come first—in our individual lives and our marriage.

Following Biblical instruction works.

Through the years, we have learned much and have also been blessed to receive sound advice that I would like to pass along to you, dear reader, in the form of 20 simple, practical steps presented in no particular order.

1. Pray together every day, faithfully.
2. Make time for each other.
3. Do what is important to your spouse, even when it is not your favorite thing to do.
4. Listen without interruption.
5. Look one another in the eye. It is hard to inflict hateful

words while looking into the eyes of someone with whom you've made memories. Don't turn your back to each other when angry. Eyes are the windows to the soul. Think about what you would do if you could no longer look into those familiar eyes. Many would give anything to gaze into the eyes of lost loved ones again.

6. Compliment often – focus on the good points. What attracted you to each other in the first place? Remind yourself and remind each other. Write a list, if necessary. What made you fall in love? Those attributes are still there—maybe hidden deep, but still there. It is worth the effort to find them.

7. Reminisce about happy times. Forget the bad. The less you rehash unpleasant memories, the more remote and unfamiliar they become.

8. Withhold criticism. Don't inflict pain into the heart of the one you love most.

9. Speak tenderly. Use a quiet tone of voice. Proverbs 15:1 says, "A soft answer turneth away wrath: but grievous words stir up anger." Hurtful words cannot be retrieved once spoken. "Kind words can be short and easy to speak, but their echoes are truly endless." *Mother Teresa*

10. Provide for each other's needs—get up and make the sandwich, pour the tea, iron the shirt, pack the lunch, find the lost watch, save each other steps.

11. Respect each other's God-given place and God-ordained capacity. Don't dominate or compete. You're not only on the same team—you **are** the team. Jesus said, "And if a house be divided against itself, that house cannot stand." (Mark 3:25) Rejoice in letting each

other shine while always pulling together toward the common goal of unity.

12. Build each other up. Steadily remind one another of past accomplishments and your faith in each other's abilities and talents. *No opinion is as valuable as that of each other.* No praise is as coveted as what comes from one another's lips.

13. Admit when you are wrong. Don't try to cover up your mess-ups.

14. Be willing to lay aside the need always to be right or say, "I told you so."

15. Take on a chore your spouse is dreading to do and accomplish it with joy.

16. Never hit one another—under no circumstances, not even in a playful way. It crosses a line that should never be passed over, and that initial respect is extremely difficult to restore.

17. Don't ever go to bed angry. Make things right, in case tomorrow never comes. "Be ye angry, and sin not: let not the sun go down upon your wrath." (Ephesians 4:26)

18. Don't bring up previous failures, hurts, and offenses. If a new disagreement arises, never bring the past into a current conversation. Deal with the issue at hand and then move on, never to bring it up again.

19. Keep a continual spirit of forgiveness in your heart. Forgive quickly and thoroughly. Always give each other the benefit of the doubt, and think the best, not worst of each other.

20. Always kiss each other goodnight.

Each day is ticking away and bringing us nearer the final crossing when we will say goodbye to those with whom we have traveled in this life. We can make the most of our journey and prevent future regrets by doing the right things today.

Keeping love alive is not difficult. It starts with saying "I love you" often and sincerely, then doing everything in your power to prove that it's true.

50

OUR LEGACY

"And these words, which I command thee this day, shall be in thine heart: and thou shalt teach them diligently unto thy children, and shalt talk of them when thou sittest in thine house, and when thou walkest by the way, and when thou liest down, and when thou risest up." Deuteronomy 6:6,7

Each one of us is building a legacy that will outlive our time on earth. Each day we live and breathe, we are writing our life's story and leaving fingerprints and footprints everywhere we go—evidence that we have been here and touched the lives of those with whom we sojourn. We pass in and out of some people's lives, never to leave more than a fleeting impression that is soon forgotten. Others who are closer to us and with whom we have more interaction will be more profoundly influenced and affected by who we are and what we do. What kind of legacy will we leave? How will we be remembered?

In their book, "The Hand that Rocks the Cradle," Sharilyn Martin and Sue Hooley relate the following story that I share with their permission.

"Come with me to an old farmhouse where a mother kneels in prayer. Tears flow as she cries out to God for strength to go on for the sake of her three little ones. If only her husband would be a Godly man and a spiritual leader! Although he provides the material needs of his family, his neglect of their emotional and spiritual needs is a burden that threatens to crush her. The flame of faith burns feebly tonight, and she feels like giving up. Is the struggle worth it?

Go with me, fifty years later, to a softly lighted chapel where the woman's wasted body now lies in a coffin. Her children, adults now, speak reverently of the mother who provided a guiding light through their formative years, drawing them to their own faith in her Savior. A score of young Christian men and women look lovingly on their grandmother's face. Tomorrow her grandsons will carry her to her grave. Tomorrow they will sing of a praying mother and a grandma who loved Jesus.

Was the struggle worth it?

My imagination pushes the fast-forward button of time, and another fifty years slip by. In my mind's eye, I see another coffin in the chapel – not my grandmother's, but mine. The little ones that snuggle in my arms today will then be grown men and women with families of their own. What will the picture look like?

Today I am painting that picture of tomorrow. Today the colors are wet in my hands, but tomorrow they will have dried. What kind of legacy will I leave?"

It is sobering to think about how Zach will remember his mama when I have passed off the scene. Will I leave behind the legacy of a praying mother? Will he remember seeing in me a servant's heart? Will memories of my life lived before him day by day bring recollections of godliness, holy living, and kind deeds?

Sometimes, we think they aren't paying attention, and it isn't all that important to get our own spiritual needs met so we can pass on a Godly legacy to them. We could not be more wrong in thinking this way. If you and I don't train by example and instill in their impressionable hearts a true love and respect for God, who will? The public school system? Television and the entertainment world? The music they listen to or the movies they watch? Can you feel and sense the disdain for holiness in our modern world as a whole?

Mothers have a tremendous responsibility. The actual weight of the power of persuasion we hold over our husbands and children can never be measured and should never be underestimated. We have the ability in our hands to make all the difference, whether good or bad.

Are we teaching our children to love this world more than to treasure their eternal soul? Are we so intent on their outward appearance that we are overlooking their spiritual welfare? Do we push them to excel in material gain yet never warn them that there is a God and a Judgment Day is coming where we will have to meet Him and give full accountability of our lives lived on earth? What is our example teaching our children? The example we are setting today is permanently etching the legacy we will one day leave behind.

I am extremely blessed to have a Godly husband who cares as strongly as I about Zach's spiritual welfare. The dear woman in the article above did not have that support, yet, she plodded on, by God's strength and grace, and kept the torch of truth lit in front of her children, who later picked it up and carried it forward after her death.

I am also abundantly blessed to have been raised around a family altar. Each night, Mom, Dad, and I gathered together to read the Bible and pray. Kevin and I now carry on that tradition in our own home, and one of my favorite parts of each day is when the three of us gather at night to have family worship. We love reading the Bible or a sound, Godly book together, and then we pray. I hope Zach will look back and cherish these memories with Kevin and me as much as I treasure my memories of family altar times with Mom and Dad.

How we live in front of our children will have eternal, never-ending repercussions. We can't undo the past or go back and remake already made choices, but we can, by God's grace, **become** the person we want to be remembered as—starting today, beginning now. Someday, may each of our children be able to say along with the Psalmist, David, "The lines are fallen unto me in pleasant *places*; yea, I have a goodly heritage." (Psalm 16:6)

Our legacy is now in the making. Fast-forward to your own funeral, and imagine seeing your family's faces as they gather around your body that one last time—what do you want the picture to look like? How do you want to be remembered?

Made in the USA
Middletown, DE
04 September 2021